Mary, Lady Chudleigh

Shearsman Classics, Vol. 4

Other titles in the *Shearsman Classics* series:

1. Poets of Devon and Cornwall, *from Barclay to Coleridge*
2. Robert Herrick: *Selected Poems*
3. Spanish Poetry of the Golden Age, *in contemporary English translations*

Forthcoming in the same series:

5. William Strode: *Selected Poems*
6. Sir Thomas Wyatt: *Selected Poems*

Mary, Lady Chudleigh

Selected Poems

Edited by Julie Sampson

Shearsman Books
Exeter

Published in the United Kingdom in 2009 by
Shearsman Books Ltd
58 Velwell Road
Exeter EX4 4LD

ISBN 978-1-84861-048-4
First Edition

Selection, introduction and notes
copyright © Julie Sampson, 2009.

The right of Julie Sampson to be identified as the author of the
introduction and the notes to this work has been
asserted by her in accordance with the
Copyrights, Designs and Patents Act of 1988.
All rights reserved.

Contents

Introduction	6
To the Queens Most Excellent Majesty	21
On the Death of his Highness the Duke of Glocester	22
On the Vanities of this Life	33
To Almystrea	39
To Clorissa	40
To Mr Dryden, on his excellent Translation of Virgil	43
Song	45
To Eugenia	46
The Wish	48
Elevation	48
Friendship	49
The Happy Man	50
To the Ladies	51
To the Queen's most Excellent Majesty	52
The Resolution	56
A Pindarick Ode	74
To the Learn'd and Ingenious Dr. Musgrave of Exeter	77
The Observation	80
Solitude	82
On the Death of my Honoured Mother Mrs. Lee	85
On the Death of my dear Daughter Eliza Maria Chudleigh	91
The Offering	95
The Resolve	99
One of Lucian's Dialogues of the Dead Paraphras'd	100
To the Queen's most Excellent Majesty	104
from The Song of the Three Children Paraphras'd	108
from The Ladies Defence	111
Notes on Text and Sources	123
Notes to the Poems	123
Selected Bibliography	143

Introduction

If Mary, Lady Chudleigh, who died in 1710, had known of the exploits of her granddaughter Elizabeth, 39 years later, she might have turned in her grave. For Chudleigh's work had an imperative moral intent, particularly directed at other women, who she advocated should become skilled in the realms of self-discipline and inner containment; not for her the C18 cult of celebrity in which, by contrast, Elizabeth seemed to wish to immerse herself. Chudleigh's poetry embodied the spirit of the poetical age in its eliciting of the pastoral or retreat style, spiced with a dose of classicism and academic rigour. Elizabeth, on the other hand, apparently revelled in flaunting the very qualities her grandmother had so deplored and despised—three centuries later there is more documentation to be found about her than her more conventionally talented grandmother.

In 1749, Elizabeth—then a maid of honour to the Princess of Wales—made her first startling appearance before the C18 media circus, which duly reported how she had presented herself at Court as though "undressed for sacrifice ... she wore a smile, some foliage rather low round her middle and a covering of the flimsiest flesh-coloured gauze". Correspondents noted how Princess Augusta had thrown her veil over the girl after, disguised as Ipighenia, she had appeared at a court masquerade in transparent muslin and apparently topless. A few years later, after she had become the Duchess of Kingston, Elizabeth's notoriety increased when she became the first and only woman to be tried for bigamy. Infamy followed her after her death when several writers—including Thackeray—introduced her as a character in their novels.

Perhaps then Mary, Lady Chudleigh's reactions to her wayward granddaughter would have been tempered by a certain admiration, for, if nothing else, Elizabeth seems to have inherited her ancestor's commitment to women's self-determination, in the face of a patriarchal cultural climate. Interestingly, although Elizabeth was said to be too impatient to apply herself to study and education, she seems to have written an account of her own life, even mentioning her grandmother.

Elizabeth was the daughter of Lady Chudleigh's second son, Thomas. What is known directly of Mary Chudleigh's life comes from another branch of her family and other granddaughters, who were offspring of George, her eldest son and the fourth Baron. They must have been rather more conventional women than their cousin, as there is scant information to be found on their lives; one of them however did write a kind of memoir of her grandmother for the C18 biographer George Ballard, which was published in 1752, in his *Memoirs of Several Ladies of Great Britain*.

Recent trends in literary criticism tend to abandon interest in a writer's life, preferring instead textual and contextual analysis; in the case of Mary Chudleigh, however, some awareness of archival records does enhance an interpretative understanding of the poems, even if the facts need to be considered with an open mind. Until recently the apparent solitariness of the poet's life—her supposedly unhappy marriage and reclusive style of living—attracted critical attention, but these assumptions are now being questioned. Some of her letters and essays do seem to confirm the isolated nature of her life; for instance, writing to her friend Elizabeth Thomas, in 1703, Chudleigh tells her that "The greatest Part of my time is spent in my Closet" and that there "I find my Books and my Thoughts to be the most agreeable Companions". This could indicate that, as she grew older, and increasingly disabled with the rheumatic condition that eventually killed her, the poet withdrew from the vibrant social and familial circles that had sustained her, into the self-containment of an absorbing inner world; perhaps it was from this apparently solitary period that she drew material for her poems and essays. Her so-called seclusion did not in any case detract from the growing fame and acclaim that Chudleigh began to receive after the publication of her first volume, in 1701. Her letters show that she travelled to London towards the end of her life, suggesting that, until her illness, she had been an active member of society. Also, during these last years, she spent the winters in Exeter because, as she wrote to Thomas, "Ashton is healthy enough in the Summer but I cannot be here in the Winter without hazarding my life".

Chudleigh's tendency to withdraw from the world would in any case be unsurprising for, from a very early age, she had lost a number of loved family members. Even in a time when deaths of close family members were always to be expected, the losses she suffered do seem excessive, and perhaps provide an explanation for the often melancholic and meditative tone of her work. After the poet's own birth in 1656, the oldest, and longest-surviving child of Richard and Maria Lee, Mary (or Maria), would have been painfully aware of the death of her five-year-old brother William when she was eleven, and her baby sister Martha, when she was sixteen. Mary's other brother Richard did live to be an adult, but was twenty years her junior and died at the age of twenty-five. After the writer married and had a family, the bereavements continued. Of her own children, only two survived to adulthood: George, born 1683, and Thomas, born 1687. Her daughter, also Mary, born two years after the writer's marriage in 1674, died before she was a year old; her son Richard, born 1685, died at the age of three. The cruellest of all the losses was perhaps that of her second daughter Eliza, at the age of 9 or 10, in 1701/2, probably of smallpox; the agony of this experience is described—as is the death of the poet's own mother—in the moving poems *On the Death of my Honoured Mother, Mrs Lee, On the Death of my dear Daughter Eliza Maria Chudleigh* and *To the Learn'd and Ingenious Dr Musgrave of Exeter*.

Counterbalancing and perhaps relieving the traumas of these deaths, Mary Chudleigh did have extensive and complicated family networks, as well as extended social and literary contacts within which to interact and foster her writing career—first as a writer of manuscripts which could be shared and exchanged with others within a coterie or group, and in later life as a well-known and respected poet and essayist.

Both sides of the poet's family had strong West-country roots. The Sydenhams, her mother Mary's family, were active Parliamentarians and puritans from Wynford Eagle in Dorset. Several of Mary Sydenham's nine siblings gained public acclaim. Col. William Sydenham, later Governor of the Isle of Wight, fought for Parliament in the Civil War and became a member of Oliver Cromwell's council; after the Restoration he was considered to be one of the twelve most dangerous men in the kingdom. Dr Thomas Sydenham also fought for Cromwell and gained respect and recognition for his medical works. His friends included several men who are likely to have been fruitful contacts for his niece: these included the philosopher John Locke and the scientist Richard Boyle. The most notorious event that affected the Sydenhams in Mary's mother's lifetime was however the brutal murder of her own mother (the poet's grandmother—another Mary), at her home in Wynford Eagle, by a troop of Royalists during the Civil War. Mary Chudleigh's own fated encounters with death followed closely that of her mother, who had been only twelve at the time.

Chudleigh's bond with her mother seems to have been close; such is suggested by the poem about her. A similar attachment is suggested with Richard Lee, her father, who was probably responsible for his daughter's thorough education. He apparently accompanied her on social visits; one of these was to her cousins in Dorset, just after her marriage. Richard was son of William Lee of Pinhoe, who had married Jane Michell of Topsham; the Lees were men of property with an estate at Winslade, in the parish of Clyst St George, near Exeter. Richard was elected M.P. for Barnstaple several times; he was also actively involved in local puritan circles.

With her marriage at Clyst St George, in March 1674, Mary Lee was introduced into another extended circle of cultured West-country people: the Chudleighs from Ashton, and their cousins the Cliffords from nearby Ugbrooke Park. The Chudleigh family had held Place Barton at Ashton since the C14 and were patrons and benefactors of Ashton church. George, Mary's husband, who became the 3rd Baronet in 1691 upon the death of his father (also George), seems to have been some twenty years older than his wife. According to one source he had matriculated at Oxford in 1653, just three years before her birth and in 1656, the year she was born, was admitted into the Inner Temple. Little more is known of him or his life and until recently all the writings on the poet present him as a difficult man; however the inference that the Chudleighs' marriage was unhappy has no basis in fact, but has been assumed from her poem 'The Ladies Defence' and from the content of one or two letters.

Although his father and grandfather seem to have been esteemed men, the Chudleigh family's involvements in the tempestuous religious and political affairs of the mid-1600s were more chequered and complicated than those of either the Lees or the Sydenhams. During the early years of the Civil War George Chudleigh, 1st Baronet, (grandfather to Mary's husband) was an active Parliamentarian; his son James however (her husband's uncle), a Parliamentarian major-general, seems to have brought disgrace upon his family: he was accused of treachery after being defeated and captured in 1643, at the Battle of Stratton, where he had reputedly gone over to the Royalists. Consequently, his father also came under suspicion and that may be the reason that he changed his allegiance to the Royalists during the same year. Place, at Ashton, the Chudleigh home, where Mary moved with her family in 1688, had been garrisoned by the King, but was afterwards taken by Fairfax as a Parliamentarian outpost.

After her marriage, and especially after the move to the family seat, Mary Chudleigh was introduced into a rich literary network. Some of her sisters-in-law may have been participants in her coteries, and it is likely that the poet was surrounded by a community of culturally interested women, for several in this extended family network lived in the vicinity. These included George's sister Elizabeth Hunt, who lived at Hams, a manor-house near Chudleigh: she died in 1708, and her memorial at Ashton church suggests that she remained close to her birth family. Several people in the Chudleigh family had literary inclinations, including George's uncle, John Chudleigh, who was a poet—he wrote an 'Elegy' on Donne, published in 1635. Through his aunt (also Mary Chudleigh), the 3rd Baronet was first cousin to Sir Thomas Clifford, High Treasurer to Charles II, member of the Cabal and 1st Baron of Ugbrooke; the many cousins of that family would have been within reach of Ashton for social and cultural occasions. Thomas Clifford had died in 1673, a year before the Chudleighs' marriage, but his large family of over 15 children were the same generation as Mary Chudleigh and the Cliffords were known for their artistic interests. Hugh Clifford, the 2nd Baron (born 1663), married Anne Preston who seems to have had some literary skills, for she compiled a *Pharmacopæia* in 1690.

The most famous and influential of the literary contacts that Mary developed through her Ugbrooke associations was that with

Dryden, who was a frequent visitor to the estate as a friend of Lord Clifford and who, legend has it, translated his volume of Virgil whilst seated at his favourite spot there—now called Dryden's Seat. His translations of Virgil and other classical writers were essential reading for Mary Chudleigh, his protégée, whose poems display a sophisticated understanding and knowledge of the classics. Dryden became the most important of Chudleigh's male supporters or patrons; others included the Platonist John Norris.

Chudleigh's work would have circulated in manuscript form amongst local family and literary circles before the publication of the first volumes of poetry—*The Ladies Defence* (1701), which was printed anonymously, and *Poems on Several Occasions* (1703). After these publications Chudleigh's work attracted a much wider audience, and she drew attention and acclaim from a broader network of women writers, including Elizabeth Thomas and Mary Astell. Several of her female acquaintances are embedded within the classical and pastoral pen-names used in some of the poems. Some of these names have been identified: Chudleigh employed the name *Marissa* for herself; *Corinna* was Elizabeth Thomas; *Philinda* was Chudleigh's mother, and *Almystrea* was Mary Astell. Others remain unknown: as yet, for instance, no one has identified *Cleanthe*, *Clorissa*, *Lucinda* or *Eugenia*.

Because of the intimacy and intensity of some of the poems that are explicitly directed to individual—but secretly encoded—friends, some have written of Chudleigh as the "English Sappho". This tribute was ascribed to her shortly soon after she died, for there is at least one dedication to her as "Sappho Anglicana", by the Exeter scholar John Reynolds, who dedicated a map of Europe to her in 1711. At present there is no evidence of any connections she may have had with other women writing in the South-West, apart from those provided by her family and acquaintances, but it is possible that she may have known—or known of—the following writers: Elizabeth Polwhele (writer of the comedy *The Frolics*) who probably came from Cornwall or Devon; Delarivière Manley, who as a young woman lived in Devon and retired to Exeter in 1696, and Priscilla Cotton, who wrote the first female defence of women's preaching when she was imprisoned in Exeter, in 1656.

Mary, Lady Chudleigh was one of a network of women who were feeling their way into the climate of post-Restoration engagement with gender issues: exploration (of concerns related to gender difference) and experimentation (with genres and modes of writing) were typical; the poet-essayist's proto-feminist writings have naturally brought her to the attention of recent critics. The emphasis on Chudleigh's apparent preoccupation with women's affairs is due to the popularity of her most anthologised poem 'To the Ladies' and to the privileging of her first publication, *The Ladies Defence* (which appears in several anthologies). However, the reading of Chudleigh's work that I would like to encourage goes beyond her proto-feminist issues—although it implicitly assimilates these—and stresses instead her wider philosophical ambition to endorse and encourage an integration of mind, body and spirit, which transcends any specific or narrow concern with contemporary gender issues. Hers is a much broader remit: as well as re-thinking women's affairs it takes on current religious debates and, beyond that, meditates on and questions the responsibilities of the individual self and soul in the context of a rapidly changing society. Chudleigh is quite radical in a quiet way, but it is easy to miss this and be taken in by the surface conventionality: she has been read as a conforming Tory and as a dedicated Royalist, but there are hidden agendas to be found below and beyond the smoke-screen of the outer text. Her choice of form and genre may also seem predictable. She uses forms such as the lyric, the prose meditation, or the ode then in vogue and wraps them up in the language of the pastoral or retreat mode—a literary tradition with classical origins, in which writers focused on idealised rural subjects. C17 and early C18 women writers made use of the pastoral genre as a vehicle that could express a feminised poetics. Chudleigh richly contextualises her poetry with classical references: the total effect is of predictable themes and subjects, which disguise more challenging content bubbling beneath the surface.

In 'The Resolution' for example there are frequent references to male exemplars from the C17 writing canon: they rampage through the poem; but a careful reading will then begin to take in the—at first insipid and infrequent—allusions to particular women in history, and then notice that these female-figures are meticulously positioned in the poem so that they function as a sub-text, a hidden foregrounding beneath the conventional canonical listings of the upper text. The poem seems to profess deference towards the more famous and influential male writers, but Chudleigh's documentation of commendable characters from ancient history implicitly emphasises female, rather than male personalities. Although the list of men is more numerous, the women who appear tend to evoke a more charged and detailed, even persona-identified narrative; for example, Arria and especially Lucretia are quintessential in their goodness, courage and consummate greatness: thus the poet subverts the norm and encodes a privileging of female her-story.

Admittedly, it is tempting to skim over the dense textual allusions, yet without the assimilation of at least some of these, the richer tapestry of the poems may not be revealed. Take for example the first poem in *Poems*, 'On the Death of the Duke of Glocester': after a lengthy preamble about the speaker's decision to leave the corrupted outer world, the poet/persona begins by establishing her idyllic Arcadian world, her "little safe Retreat", using the linguistic conventions of the retreat mode; she is in ecstasy, choosing to "my Books and Thoughts entirely live", stating her poetic commitment and a pledge to inner serenity. Her choice of ideal site is supported by her own muse: "The Muse well pleas'd, my choice approv'd". At this height of pastoral bliss the first classical reference appears, as "Sad Philomela sung her Pains". "Philomela" encodes several interrelated meanings, all of which enhance and complicate the interpretation of the surface text: "nightingale" was often used to figure specifically the woman poet; that was probably the inherent meaning of the name (embodying sweetness and reclusiveness) as used for a pseudonym by the poet Elizabeth Singer-Rowe, whose poems were published in 1696. Possibly Chudleigh's Philomela is intended to refer directly to Rowe. In Ovid's myth Philomela was raped by her sister Procne's husband Tereus and after he imprisoned her and cut out her tongue she wove her story into a tapestry; her eventual fate was to be transformed into a nightingale. Given the density and specificity of Chudleigh's later classical allusions Philomela's significance (as the first mythological reference of the collection) carries with it the weight, darkness and transformative healing of its mythological connotations.

There is a suggestion of the persona's self-identification with Philomela in lines 92–5 and there are several meeting points between poem, poet and Philomela's story—from the enclosed forest-retreat of Philomela's prison and site of the poet's idyll, to the state of impasse brought about by intense pain. Indeed the opening poem matches, in miniature, the movement of the whole collection of poems, progressing from a statement of deep personal affect (pain, loss, hidden torments, past wrongs) to a reckoning, release of song (poetry) and acceptance, towards a mode of inner-reconciliation and affirmation. The poet-persona, as wounded Philomela, is "weaving" her "story", as lyric-poetry, to present a completed "tapestry" to take to her "sister", the Queen, as one of a community of like-minded female sisters.

As well as voicing the writer's concerns on the position of women in her society, the poetry encodes Chudleigh's views on the religious debates of her day. Whereas she has until recently been understood as a conforming Anglican—agreeing with the Royalist and conformist proclivities of her husband's family—one critic, Barbara Olive, has suggested that the poet's work expresses what she calls a "conforming dissent": whilst claiming allegiance to the Protestant church, the poet's writings promote a hidden agenda, which foregrounds further reforming changes from within the texts. Olive's insights about 'Song of the Three Children Paraphras'd', from the perspective of its "Restoration Puritanism", are particularly insightful. Of course as a West-country poet, with her own complicated familial relationship to the church, and the several notable events of her day, Chudleigh's tendency to be covert about her own underlying faith is understandable. (Such events would include the Popish Plot and Monmouth's Rebellion, both in the 1680s, as well as the Glorious Revolution, 1688.) It was a time when local people learned to be duplicitous in their response to frequent changes.

The writer's sources are many and varied, and match her extensive education. Although her reading of the classics was always in translation, she was—according to her granddaughter's memoir—

"addicted to reading", and kept up with contemporary theories in philosophy, science, ancient history, natural history and archaeology; the memoir notes that her "beloved studies" were "poetry and history". Not only familiar with many of the current writers of poetry, verse translation and drama, Chudleigh's prose and poetry engages with Neoplatonism, as well as with recent discoveries in science, which developed in part from the Neoplatonic interest in natural theology. For example, she is familiar with the work of Thomas Burnet, whose writings instigated a flurry of discussion amongst C17 philosophers regarding the integration of theological understanding with theories of natural phenomena. Chudleigh's fascination with natural scientific observations can be seen in such poems as 'Solitude' and 'The Offering', which contain images of the "dancing atoms" derived from Epicurean thought about the atomic structure of matter: her poems indicate her attempt to synchronise scientific, philosophical and theological understandings and to create what Ezell labels a "rational theology" or "song of science".

The overarching theme in Mary Chudleigh's poetry however is not indebted to any one branch of knowledge; instead it concentrates on the individual's responsibility to learn to control conflicting emotions. She is instructing women "for whom they [the poems] are chiefly design'd"—though her comments imply that men are also in her thoughts—as to their need and ability to find interior resources of strength and resolution. In her preface to the *Poems on Several Occasions*, the poet recommends a reconciliation between inner and outer conflicts, a turning away from bodily and sensual experiences towards heightened spiritual awareness, thus moving the individual beyond pain and torment; the ultimate aim is to reach a state of complete self-sufficiency: "The way to be truly easie, to be always serene, to have our Passions under a due Government, to be wholly our own . . . is to retire into our selves, to live upon our own Stock".

The poems reach toward religious acceptance and tolerance in the face of difference and conflict; they remark universally on how individuals can live harmoniously in a dissolute society; they advise how a woman can use her intelligence and reading as a means of self-instruction and transformation to allow her progress towards independent resolution and moral self-government. Rather than feeling repressed, suppressed and submissive, the woman's renewed sense of ethical integrity will allow a relationship towards others that will be directed from an inner position of serenity and calm self-control. Chudleigh calls this state a "happy disposition of mind".

If this sounds familiar to C21 readers it is not surprising. Once the reader has adapted to the C17 verbal differences, several of these poems resonate with modern self-improvement books that promote the individual's need to self-determine one's life. This is because the traditions of self-governance advocated by such behavioural therapies as CBT (cognitive behavioural therapy) are developed from the classical Stoics—especially Epictetus, whose *Enchiridion* exemplifies methods of internalising the rules of individual self-control. Chudleigh's work is peppered with Epictetan concepts. She makes at least two explicit references to him—in the preface to *The Ladies Defence* and in 'The Resolution'. Her directives to women make use of his principles of moral corrective, emphasising both their ability to train their own emotions towards a state of inner containment and also their ambition to improve their intellectual abilities through reading. She says: "the Books I would chiefly recommend, next to the Sacred Scriptures and Devotional Discourses, are Seneca's *Morals*, together with those of Plutarch and the Philosophy of Epictetus". A dose of Mary Chudleigh's poetry may perhaps be as beneficial as reading the latest self-help manual.

Chudleigh appears to have found for herself the inner place of solace and self-containment which she recommends to her readers; in one letter to Elizabeth Thomas in 1701, she refers to a local event which could have caused her anxiety and concern: "there was seen here very lately a great circle round the Sun, which frighted the people of Exeter . . . but things of this kind never disturb me", and in a letter two years later she tells her friend that when alone in her closet "I meet with nothing to disturb me, nothing to render me uneasy".

As well as poetry Chudleigh wrote a series of meditative *Essays on Several Subjects* which were dedicated to Sophia, Electress of Hanover and published in 1710, shortly before the poet's death in December that year. The essays complemented and extended her poetic *oeuvre* and are worth seeking out for their meditative philosophical explorations of varying states of inner awareness (including Pride, Humility and Fear) and examinations of human relationships (including Friendship, Love and Justice); they are especially useful for the detailed reading lists which the writer recommends for her female readership.

It is not known when Chudleigh wrote individual poems, but Margaret Ezell considers that she probably began writing early in her life, as this is suggested in one or two family letters. It is possible that the poems published in the present collection were written at various times; notwithstanding this, my reading of *Poems on Several Occasions* chimes with Ezell's comment that they "constitute ... a continuous philosophical exploration of human passions". Whatever the chronology of individual poems, it is likely that the poet ordered and placed them within the volume so as to trace a process. *Poems on Several Occasions* is dedicated to Queen Anne and three panegyrics structure the collection, marking its beginning, middle and end; in the centre, a place of focus, is the long and complex 'The Resolution'; finally, the emotional tone of the collection reads as though marking a progression, from a persona speaking from an objective stance, towards a climax of deeply emotive and personal poems; this concludes with a sequence expressing a state of reconciliation and resolution.

It is felicitous to finish here with an image of Mary, Lady Chudleigh seated in a rose-scented arbour at her private retreat at Place Barton, and penning her poems away from the hustle and bustle of C17 London. In her preface to the poems the poet remarks that her readers will "find a Picture of my Mind, my sentiments all laid open to their View". The pastoral idyll established at the beginning of the first poem has already been noted: how "cool was the place and quiet was the mind". At that period "Place was an outstanding house—a very extensive courtyard mansion with gatehouse and arch and large deer park of about 300 acres"; not only did it have "two large fishponds" but a "C17 formal garden", laid out in a "number of terraces". According to recent evidence, this was a rare survival. Perhaps then, this Devonian writer had a real countryside location in which to write; her poems, with their emphasis on the delights and contentment of pastoral retreat, are not just to be read within that mode of poetic rhetoric, but also as representations of an idyllic rural situation, which we, from our C21 perspective, can recreate in our minds. The scene brings home the personal, that poetic intimacy and immediacy which can so easily be destroyed in the face of intense analysis and is a reminder that, as with contemporary C21—and indeed any—poetry, it is good to just read, imagine, contemplate.

Julie Sampson
January 2009

To The Queen's Most Excellent Majesty

MADAM,

'Tis not without awful Thoughts and a trembling Hand that these Poems are laid at your Royal Feet. The Address has too much Confidence; the Ambition is too aspiring; But to whom should a Woman unknown to the World, and who has not Merit enough to defend her from the Censure of Criticks, fly for Protection, but to Your *Majesty?* The Greatest, the Best, and the most Illustrious Person of Your Sex and Age.

That wonderful Condescension, that surprizing Humility, and admirable Sweetness of Temper, which induc'd Your *Majesty* to accept a Congratulatory Ode on Your happy Accession to the Crown, give Ground to hope that from a Goodness and Generosity boundless as Yours, I may promise my self both Pardon and Protection, who am, with the profoundest Veneration,

MADAM, Your Majesty's most Loyal, most Humble, and most Obedient Servant,

MARY CHUDLEIGH.

On the Death of his Highness the Duke of Glocester

1.

I'le take my Leave of Business, Noise and Care,
   And trust this stormy Sea no more:
   Condemn'd to Toil, and fed with Air,
I've often sighing look'd towards the Shore:
   And when the boistrous Winds did cease,   5
   And all was still, and all was Peace,
   Afraid of Calms, and flatt'ring Skies,
On the deceitful Waves I fixt my Eyes,
And on a sudden saw the threatning Billows rise:
   Then trembling beg'd the Pow'rs Divine,   10
Some little safe Retreat might be for ever mine:
   O give, I cry'd, where e'er you please,
   Those Gifts which Mortals prize,
   Grown fond of Privacy and Ease,
I now the gaudy Pomps of Life despise.   15
   Still let the Greedy strive with Pain,
   T'augment their shining Heaps of Clay;
   And punish'd with the Thirst of Gain,
   Their Honour lose, their Conscience stain:
   Let th'ambitious Thrones desire   20
   And still with guilty hast aspire;
   Thro' Blood and Dangers force their Way,
   And o'er the World extend their Sway,
While I my time to nobler Uses give,
And to my Books, and Thoughts entirely live;   25
Those dear Delights, in which I still shall find
   Ten thousand Joys to feast my Mind,
Joys, great as Sense can bear, from all its Dross refin'd.

2.

   The Muse well pleas'd, my choice approv'd,
   And led me to the Shades she lov'd: 30
   To Shades, like those first fam'd Abodes
   Of happy Men, and rural Gods;

Where, in the World's blest Infant State,
   When all in Friendship were combin'd
   And all were just, and all were kind; 35
   E're glitt'ring Show'rs, dispers'd by *Jove,*
   And Gold were made the Price of Love,
   The Nymphs and Swains did bless their Fate,
   And all their mutual Joys relate,
   Danc'd and sung, and void of Strife. 40
   Enjoy'd all Harmless Sweets of Life;
While on their tuneful Reeds their Poets play'd,
And their chast Loves to future Times convey'd.

             3.
Cool was the place, and quiet as my Mind,
   The Sun cou'd there no Entrance find: 45
   No ruffling Winds the Boughs did move:
   The Waters gently crept along,
   As with their flowry Banks in Love:
   The Birds with soft harmonious Strains,
      Did entertain my Ear; 50
   Sad *Philomela* sung her Pains,
      Express'd her Wrongs, and her Despair;
   I listen'd to her mournful Song,
      The charming Warbler pleas'd,
And I, me thought, with new Delight was seiz'd: 55
Her Voice with tender'st Passions fill'd my Breast,
And I felt Raptures not to be express'd;
   Raptures, till that soft Hour unknown,
   My Soul seem'd from my Body flown:
Vain World, said I, take, take my last adieu, 60
I'le to my self, and to my Muse be true,
And never more phantastick Forms pursue:
Such glorious Nothings let the Great adore,
   Let them their airy *Juno's* court,
      I'le be deceiv'd no more, 65
   Nor to the Marts of Fame resort:
From this dear Solitude no more remove,
But here confine my Joy, my Hope, my Love.

4.

Thus were my Hours in Extasies employ'd,
And I the secret Sweets of Life enjoy'd: 70
Serene, and calm, from every Pressure free,
Inslav'd alone by flatt'ring Poesie:
But Oh! how pleasing did her Fetters prove!
How much did I, th' endearing Charmer Love!
No former Cares durst once my Soul molest, 75
No past Unkindness discompos'd my Breast;
All was forgot, as if in *Lethe's* Stream
I'd quench'd my Thirst, the past was all a Dream:
But as I pleas'd my self with this unenvy'd state,
    Behold! a wondrous Turn of Fate! 80
    A hollow Melancholy Sound
    Dispers'd an awful Horror round,
And hideous Groans thro' all the Grove resound
    Nature the dismal Noise did hear,
    Nature her self did seem to fear: 85
The bleating Flocks lay trembling on the Plains;
    The Brooks ran murmuring by,
And Echo to their Murmurs made reply:
The lofty Trees their verdant Honours shake;
The frighted Birds with hast their Boughs forsake, 90
And for securer Seats to distant Groves repair.
The much wrong'd *Philomel* durst now no more
    Her former Injuries deplore;
    Forgot were all her moving Strains
    Forgot each sweet melodious Air; 95
The weaker Passion, Grief, surrendred to her Fear.

5.

A sudden Gloom its dusky Empire spread,
And I was seiz'd with an unusual dread:
Where e'er I look'd, each Object brought affright:
And I cou'd only mournful Accents hear, 100
Which from th'adjacent Hills did wound my Ear;
Th'adjacent Hills the gen'ral Horror share:

Amaz'd I sat, depriv'd of all Delight,
The Muse was fled, fled ev'ry pleasing Thought,
And in their Room were black Ideas brought,   105
By busie Fear, and active Fancy wrought.
    At length the doleful Sound drew near,
And lo, the British Genius did appear!
        Solemn his Pace,
            Dejected were his Eyes,   110
And from his Breast thick thronging Sighs arise:
The Tears ran down his venerable Face,
And he with Lamentations loud fill'd all the sacred Place.

            6.
He's Dead he cry'd! the young, the much belov'd!
From us too soon, Ah! much too soon remov'd!   115
Snatch'd hence in his first Dawn, his Infant Bloom!
So fell *Marcellus* by a rigorous Doom.
The Good, the Great, the Joy, the Pride of *Rome*!
But Oh! he wants like him a *Maro* to rehearse
His early worth in never dying Verse: 120
To sing those rising Wonders which in him were seen;
That Morning light which did itself display,
Presaging earnest of a glorious Day;
His Face was Charming, and his Make Divine,
As if in him assembl'd did combine   125
The num'rous Graces of his Royal Line:
Such was *Ascanius,* when from flaming *Troy*
Pious *Æneas* led the lovely Boy,
And such the God when to the *Tyrian* Queen
        A welcom Guest he came;   130
And in his Shape caress'd th' illustrious Dame
And kindled in her Breast the inauspicious Flame.

            7.
But this, alas! was but th' exterior part;
    For the chief Beauties were within:
        There Nature shew'd her greatest Art,   135

  And did a Master-piece begin:
  But ah! the Strokes were much too fine,
    Too delicate to last:
Sweet was his Temper, generous his Mind,
And much beyond his Years, to Martial Arts inclin'd: 140
Averse to Softness, and for one so young,
His Sense was manly, and his Reason strong:
What e'er was taught him he would learn so fast
    As if 'twas his design
When he to full Maturity was grown, 145
  Th'applauding World amaz'd should find
   What e'er was worthy to be known,
He with the noblest Toil had early made his own.

     8.

Such, such was he, whose Loss I now lament;
O Heav'n! why was this matchless Blessing sent! 150
Why but just shewn, and then, our Grief to raise,
Cut off in the beginning of his Days!
Had you beheld th'afflicted Royal Pair
Stand by that Bed, where the dear Suff'rer lay
   To his Disease a helpless Prey, 155
And seen them gaze on the sad doubtful Strife,
Between contending Death, and strugling Life,
Observ'd those Passions which their Souls did move,
   Those kind Effects of tender'st Love;
  Seen how their Joys a while did strive 160
   To keep their fainty Hopes alive,
   But soon alas! were forc'd to yield
    To Grief and dire Despair,
    The short contested Field:
   And them in that curst Moment view'd, 165
   When by prevailing Death subdu'd,
Breathless and pale, the beauteous Victim lay,
When his unwilling Soul was forc'd away
   From that lov'd Body which it lately blest,
That Mansion worthy so divine a Guest, 170

You must have own'd, no Age could ever show
A sadder Sight, a Scene of vaster Woe.

9.

Sorrow like theirs, what Language can express!
Their All was lost, their only Happiness!
The good *Ægeus* could not more be griev'd   175
    When he the Sable Flag perceiv'd,
Than was the Prince; but we this difference find,
    The last was calmer, more resign'd,
And had the stronger, more Majestick Mind:
He knew Complaints could give him no Relief,   180
And therefore cast a Veil upon his sullen Grief;
Th'afflicted Princess could not thus controul
The tender Motions of her troubled Soul:
Unable to resist, she gave her Sorrows way,
    And did the Dictates of her Grief obey: 185
Maternal Kindness still does preference claim,
And always burns with a more ardent Flame:
But sure no Heart was ever thus opprest,
    The Load is much too great to bear;
In sad Complaints are all her Minutes spent,   190
    And she lives only to lament:
All soft Delights are Strangers to her Breast:
His unexpected Fate does all her Thoughts ingross,
And she speaks nothing but her mighty Loss.
So mourn'd *Andromache* when she beheld   195
    Astyanax expos'd to lawless Pow'r,
    Precipitated from a lofty Tow'r:
Depriv'd of Life the Royal Youth remain'd
And with the richest *Trojan* Blood the Pavement stain'd:
Speechless she gaz'd, and by her Grief impell'd,   200
Fearless amidst the *Grecian* Troops she run,
And to her panting Bosom clasp'd her mangl'd Son.

10.

As thus he spoke *Britannia* did appear,
    Attended by a Sylvan Throng,
And with her brought the River Nymphs along: 205
He's dead! he's dead! the Genius loudly cry'd,
On whose dear Life you did so much depend,
He's dead, He's dead, she mournfully reply'd:
Heav'n would not long the mighty Blessing lend:
Some envious Pow'r, who does my Greatness fear,   210
Foreseeing if he shou'd to Manhood live,
He'd glorious Proofs of wondrous Valor give:
    To distant Lands extend his Sway,
And teach remotest Nations to obey:
Resolv'd no pow'rful Art his Life should save,   215
Nor I should longer my lov'd *Gloucester* have.
No more they said, but to their Sighs gave way,
The Nymphs and Swains all griev'd no less than they.
    He's dead! he's dead! they weeping said;
In his cold Tomb the lovely Youth is laid,   220
And has too soon, alas! too soon the Laws of Fate obey'd.
No more, no more shall he these Groves adorn,
No more by him shall flow'ry Wreaths be worn:
No more, no more we now on him shall gaze,
No more divert him with our rural Lays,   225
Nor see him with a godlike Smile receive our humble Praise.
    Their loud Laments the Nereids hear,
    And full of Grief, and full of Fear,
    Their watry Beds in haste forsake;
And from their Locks the pearly Moisture shake: 230
All with one Voice the much lov'd Youth lament,
And in pathetic Strains their boundless Sorrow vent.

11.

    Upon the Ground I pensive lay;
    Complain'd and wept as much as they:
    My Country's Loss became my own,   235
    And I was void of Comfort grown.

He's dead! he's dead! with them I cry'd,
And to each Sigh, each Groan reply'd.
The *Thracian* Bard was not more mov'd,
When he had lost the Fair he lov'd;   240
When looking back to please his Sight
With all that could his Soul delight,
He saw her sink int' everlasting Night.
The Sorrows of the Princess pierc'd my Heart,
And I, me thought, felt all her Smart: 245
I wish'd I cou'd allay her Pain,
Or part of her Affliction share;
But Oh! such Wishes are in vain,
She must alone the pond'rous Burthen bear.
O Fate unjust! I then did cry,   250
Why must the young, the virtuous die!
Why in their Prime be snatch'd away,
Like beauteous Flow'rs which soon decay,
While Weeds enjoy the Warmth of each succeeding Day?

        12.
While thus I mourn'd, a sudden Light the Place o'er spread   255
Back to their genuine Night the frighted Shadows fled:
Dilating Skies disclos'd a brighter Day,
And for a glorious Form made way;
For the fam'd Guardian of our Isle:
The wondrous Vision did with Pomp descend,   260
With awful State his kind Approaches made,
And thus with an obliging Smile
To the much griev'd *Britannia* said,
No more, my much lov'd Charge, no more
Your time in useless Sorrows spend;   265
He's blest whose Loss you thus deplore:
Above he lives a Life Divine,
And does with dazling Splendor shine:
I met him on th' Æthereal Shore,
With Joy I did th' illustrious Youth embrace,   270
And led him to his God-like Race,

    Who sit inthron'd in wondrous State,
    Above the Reach of Death or fate:
    The *Caledonian* Chiefs were there,
    Who thro' the World have spread their Fame,   275
And justly might immortal Trophies claim:
    A long Descent of glorious Kings,
    Who did, and suffer'd mighty things:
    With them the *Danish* Heroes were,
    Who long had ancient Kingdoms sway'd,   280
    And been by Warlike States obey'd:
    With them they did their Honours share,
    With them refulgent Crowns did wear,
    From all their Toils at length they cease,
Blest with the Sweets of everlasting Peace.   285

        13.
Among the rest, that beauteous suff'ring Queen
Who'd all the turns of adverse Fortune seen;
Robb'd of a Crown, and forc'd to mourn in Chains,
And on a Scaffold end her num'rous Pains
    Receiv'd him with a cheerful Look,   290
And to her Arms her dearest Off-spring took:
Next came the martyr'd Prince, who liv'd to know
    The last Extremities of woe:
Expos'd unjustly to his People's hate,
He felt the Rigor of remorseless Fate.   295
    Virtue and spotless Innocence,
        Alas! are no Defence:
    They rather to the Rage expose
    Of bloody and relentless Foes:
    Too fierce they shine, too glaring bright,   300
    The Vicious cannot bear their Light.
Next came his Son, who long your Sceptre sway'd,
And whom his Subjects joyfully obey'd;
Then last of all the fair *Maria* came,
    Who lately grac'd the *British* Throne;   305
And there with a reviving Splendor shone,

    But made a short, a transient Stay,
By Death from all her Glories snatch'd away:
    How vain is Beauty, Wealth, or Fame,
How few the Trophies of a boasted Name! 310
    Death can't be brib'd, be won by none:
To Slaves and Kings a Fate a like, a like Regard is shown.

14.

All these the lovely Youth carest,
And welcom'd him to their eternal Rest:
Welcome, they said, to this our blissful Shore, 315
To never ending Joys, and Seats Divine,
To Realms where clear unclouded Glories shine,
Here you may safely stand and hear the Billows roar,
But shall be toss'd on that tempestuous Sea no more:
    No more shall grieve, no more complain, 320
    But free from Care, and free from Pain,
        With us for ever shall remain.
While thus they spoke, celestial Musick play'd,
And welcom! welcom! every Angel said:
With eager hast their Royal Guest they crown'd, 325
While welcom! welcom! echo'd all around,
And fill'd th' Æthereal Court with the loud cheerful Sound.

15.

He said; and to superior Joys return'd;
    Britannia now no longer mourn'd:
    No more the Nymphs, no more the Swains, 330
    With Lamentations fill'd the Plains:
The Muse came back, and with her brought
Each sprightly, each delightful Thought:
Kindly she rais'd me from the Ground,
    And smiling wip'd my Tears away: 335
While Joy, she said, is spread around,
And do's thro' all the Groves resound,
    Will you to Grief a Tribute pay,
And mourn for one who's far more blest,

Than those that are of Crowns possest? 340
No more, no more you must complain,
    But with *Britannia* now rejoice:
Britannia to the Choir above
    Will add her charming Voice:
Not one of all her beauteous Train 345
    But will obsequious prove;
And each will try who best can sing,
Who can the highest Praises bring;
Who best describe his happy State,
And best his present Joys relate. 350
Hark! Hark! the Birds are come again,
And each renews his sweet melodious Strain.
    Clear is the Skie, and bright the Day,
    Among the Boughs sweet Zephyrs play,
    And all are pleas'd, and all are gay. 355
    And dare you still your Grief express,
    As if you wish'd his Honours less,
And with an envious Eye beheld his Happiness?

        16.

Ah! cruel Muse, with Sighs I said,
Why do you thus your Slave upbraid? 360
    I neither at his Bliss repine;
    Nor is't my choice to disobey:
    Your Will, you know, has still been mine;
And I would now my ready def'rence pay:
But Oh! in vain I strive, in vain I try, 365
While my lov'd Princess grieves, I can't comply:
    Her Tears forbid me to rejoice,
    And when my Soul is on the Wing,
    And I would with *Britannia* sing,
        Her Sighs arrest my Voice. 370
But if once more you'd have me cheerful prove,
    And with your Shades again in Love,
Strive by your Charms to calm her troubled Mind;
Let her the Force of pow'rful Numbers find:

And by the Magick of your Verse restore 375
Her former Peace, then add Delights unknown before
Let her be blest, my Joys will soon return,
But while she grieves, I ne'er can cease to mourn.

On the Vanities of this Life: A Pindarick Ode

1.
What makes fond Man the trifle Life desire,
    And with such Ardor court his Pain?
'Tis Madness, worse than Madness, to admire
What brings Ten thousand Miseries in its Train:
To each soft moment, Hours of Care succeed, 5
    And for the Pleasures of a Day,
        With Years of Grief we pay;
So much our lasting Sorrows, our fleeting Joys exceed.
In vain, in vain, we Happiness pursue,
    That mighty Blessing is not here; 10
    That, like the false misguiding Fire,
Is farthest off, when we believe it near:
    Yet still we follow till we tire,
    And in the fatal Chase Expire:
    Each gaudy nothing which we view, 15
    We fancy is the wish'd for Prize,
Its painted Glories captivate our Eyes;
Blinded by Pride, we hug our own Mistake,
And foolishly adore that Idol which we make.

2.
Some hope to find it on the Coasts of Fame, 20
And hazard all to gain a glorious Name;
    Proud of Deformity and Scars,
They seek for Honour in the bloodiest Wars;
        On Dangers, unconcern'd, they run,
        And Death it self disdain to shun: 25

      This, the Rich with Wonder see,
          And fancy they are happier far
          Than those deluded Heroes are:
But this, alas! is their Mistake;
      They only dream that they are blest,   30
For when they from their pleasing Slumbers wake,
They'll find their Minds with Swarms of Cares opprest,
          So crouded, that no part is free
              To entertain Felicity:
      The Pain to get, and Fear to lose,   35
          Like Harpies, all their Joys devour:
          Who such a wretched Life wou'd chuse?
Or think those happy who must Fortune trust?
That fickle Goddess is but seldom just.
Exterior things can ne'er be truly good,   40
          Because within her Pow'r;
          This the wise Ancients understood,
And only wish'd for what wou'd Life sustain;
Esteeming all beyond superfluous and vain.

              3.
      Some think the Great are only blest,   45
Those God-like Men who shine above the rest:
          In whom united Glories meet,
And all the lower World pay Homage at their Feet:
On their exalted Heights they sit in State,
And their Commands bind like the Laws of Fate: 50
Their Regal Scepters, and their glitt'ring Crowns,
          Imprint an awful Fear in ev'ry Breast:
Death shoots his killing Arrows thro' their Frowns;
Their Smiles are welcom, as the Beams of Light
Were to the infant World, when first it rose from Night. 55
Thus, in the Firmament of Pow'r above,
          Each in his radiant Sphere does move,
              Remote from common View;
          Th'admiring Croud with Wonder gaze,
The distant Glories their weak Eyes amaze: 60

But cou'd they search into the Truth of Things,
Cou'd they but look into the Thoughts of Kings;
    If all their hidden Cares they knew,
Their Jealousies, their Fears, their Pain,
    And all the Troubles of their Reign, 65
They then wou'd pity those they now admire;
And with their humble State content, wou'd nothing
    more desire.

4.

If any thing like Happiness is here,
    If any thing deserves our Care,
        'Tis only by the Good possest; 70
    By those who Virtue's Laws obey,
And cheerfully proceed in her unerring Way;
Whose Souls are cleans'd from all the Dregs of Sin,
From all the base Alloys of their inferior Part,
And fit to harbour that Celestial Guest, 75
    Who ne'r will be confin'd
    But to a holy Breast.
    The pure and spotless Mind,
        Has all within
That the most boundless Wish can crave; 80
The most aspiring Temper hope to have:
    Nor needs the Helps of Art,
    Nor vain Supplies of Sense,
Assur'd of all in only Innocence.

5.

Malice and Envy, Discontent, and Pride, 85
Those fatal Inmates of the Vicious Mind,
Which into dang'rous Paths th' unthinking Guide,
Ne'er to the pious Breast admittance find.
As th' upper Region is Serene and clear,
    No Winds, no Clouds are there, 90
So with perpetual Calms the virtuous Soul is blest,
    Those Antepasts of everlasting Rest:
Like some firm Rock amidst the raging Waves

She stands, and their united force outbraves;
Contends, till from her Earthly Shackles free, 95
    She takes her flight
    Into immense Eternity,
And in those Realms of unexhausted Light,
Forgets the Pressures of her former State.
O'er-joy'd to find her self beyond the reach of Fate. 100

      6.
O happy Place! where ev'ry thing will please,
    Where neither Sickness, Fear, nor Strife,
Nor any of the painful Cares of Life,
      Will interrupt her Ease:
    Where ev'ry Object charms the Sight, 105
    And yields fresh Wonder and Delight,
    Where nothing's heard but Songs of Joy,
      Full of Extasie Divine,
    Seraphick Hymns! which Love inspire,
    And fill the Breast with sacred Fire: 110
      Love refin'd from drossy Heat,
    Rais'd to a flame sublime and great,
In ev'ry Heav'nly Face do's shine,
And each Celestial Tongue employ:
    What e'er we can of Friendship know, 115
    What e'er we Passion call below,
    Does but a weak Resemblance bear,
To that blest Union which is ever there,
Where Love, like Life, do's animate the whole,
As if it were but one blest individual Soul. 120

      7.
Such as a lasting Happiness would have,
    Must seek it in the peaceful Grave,
Where free from Wrongs the Dead remain.
    Life is a long continu'd Pain,
      A lingring slow Disease. 125
    Which Remedies a while may ease,
    But can not work a perfect Cure:

    Musick with its inchanting Lays,
    May for a while our Spirits raise,
    Honour and Wealth may charm the Sense,   130
    And by their pow'rful Influence
    May gently lull our Cares asleep;
    But when we think our selves secure,
And fondly hope we shall no future Ills endure,
        Our Griefs awake again,   135
And with redoubl'd Rage augment our Pain:
    In vain we stand on our Defence,
    In vain a constant Watch we keep,
        In vain each Path we guard;
    Unseen into our Souls they creep,   140
And when they once are there, 'tis very hard
    With all our Strength to force them thence;
Like bold Intruders on the whole they seize,
A Part will not th' insatiate Victors please.

            8.
    In vain, alas! in vain,   145
        We Reason's Aid implore,
That will but add a quicker Sense of Pain,
    But not our former Joys restore:
Those few who by strict Rules their Lives have led,
Who Reason's Laws attentively have read;   150
Who to its Dictates glad Submission pay,
And by their Passions never led astray,
Go resolutely on in its severest Way,
Could never solid Satisfaction find:
The most that Reason can, is to persuade the Mind,   155
    Its Troubles decently to bear,
And not permit a Murmur, or a Tear,
To tell th' inquiring World that any such are there:
But while we strive our Suff'rings to disown,
And blush to have our Frailties known;   160
While from the publick View our Griefs we hide,
    And keep them Pris'ners in our Breast,

We seem to be, but are not truly blest;
What like Contentment looks, is but th' Effect of Pride:
    From it we no advantage win,   165
    But are the same we were before,
The smarting Pains corrode us still within;
Confinement do's but make them rage the more:
    Upon the vital Stock they prey,
And by insensible degrees they wast our Life away.   170

          9.
In vain from Books we hope to gain Relief,
    Knowledge does but increase our Grief:
    The more we read, the more we find
Of th' unexhausted Store still left behind:
    To dig the wealthy Mine we try,   175
        No Pain, no Labour spare;
But the lov'd Treasure too profound does lie,
    And mocks our utmost Industry:
Like some inchanted Isle it does appear;
    The pleas'd Spectator thinks it near;   180
But when with wide spread Sails he makes to shore,
His Hopes are lost, the Phantom's seen no more:
Asham'd, and tir'd, we of Success despair,
    Our fruitless Studies we repent,
And blush to see, that after all our Care,   185
After whole Years on tedious Volumes spent,
    We only darkly understand
    That which we thought we fully knew;
Thro' Labyrinths we go without a Clue,
Till in the dang'rous Maze our selves we lose,   190
And neither know which Path t'avoid, or which to chuse.
From Thought to Thought, our restless Minds are tost,
Like Ship-wreck'd Mariners we seek the Land,
And in a Sea of Doubts are almost lost.
The *Phoenix* Truth wrapt up in Mists does lie,   195
Not to be clearly seen before we die;
Not till our Souls free from confining Clay,
Open their Eyes in everlasting Day.

To *Almystrea*

1.

Permit *Marissa* in an artless Lay
To speak her Wonder, and her Thanks repay:
Her creeping Muse can ne'er like yours ascend;
She has not Strength for such a towring Flight.
Your Wit, her humble Fancy do's transcend; 5
She can but gaze at your exalted Height:
Yet she believ'd it better to expose
    Her Failures, than ungrateful prove;
        And rather chose
To shew a want of Sense, than want of Love: 10
But taught by you, she may at length improve,
And imitate those Virtues she admires.
Your bright Example leaves a Tract Divine,
She sees a beamy Brightness in each Line,
And with ambitious Warmth aspires, 15
Attracted by the Glory of your Name,
To follow you in all the lofty Roads of Fame.

2.

Merit like yours, can no Resistance find,
But like a Deluge overwhelms the Mind;
    Gives full Possession of each Part, 20
Subdues the Soul, and captivates the Heart.
Let those whom Wealth, or Interest unite,
    Whom Avarice, or Kindred sway
    Who in the Dregs of Life delight;
And ev'ry Dictate of their Sense obey, 25
Learn here to love at a sublimer Race,
To wish for nothing but exchange of Thoughts,
    For intellectual Joys,
    And Pleasures more refin'd
Than Earth can give, or Fancy can create. 30
Let our vain Sex be fond of glitt'ring Toys,
Of pompous Titles, and affected Noise,

Let envious Men by barb'rous Custom led
      Descant on Faults,
         And in Detraction find 35
Delights unknown to a brave gen'rous Mind,
While we resolve a nobler Path to tread,
    And from Tyrannick Custom free,
View the dark Mansions of the mighty Dead,
    And all their close Recesses see; 40
      Then from those awful Shades retire,
        And take a Tour above,
      And there, the shining Scenes admire,
        Th' Opera of eternal Love;
View the Machines, on the bright Actors gaze, 45
Then in a holy Transport, blest Amaze,
To the great Author our Devotion raise,
And let our Wonder terminate in Praise.

To *Clorissa*

1.

To your lov'd Bosom pleas'd *Marissa* flies;
That place where sacred Friendship gives a Right,
    And where ten thousand Charms invite.
Let others Pow'r and awful Greatness prize;
Let them exchange their Innocence and Fame 5
For the dear Purchase of a mighty Name:
Let greedy Wretches hug their darling Store,
The tempting Produce of their Toils adore,
And still with anxious Souls, desire and grasp at more:
While I disdain to have my Bliss confin'd 10
To things which Fortune can bestow, or take,
    To things so foreign to the Mind,
And which no part of solid Pleasure make:
    Those Joys of which I am possest
    Are safely lodg'd within my Breast, 15

Where like deep Waters, undisturb'd they flow,
And as they pass, a glassy smoothness show:
Unmov'd by Storms, or by th' Attacks of Fate,
I envy none, nor wish a happier State.

2.

When all alone in some belov'd Retreat, 20
Remote from Noise, from Bus'ness, and from Strife,
Those constant curst Attendants of the Great;
I freely can with my own Thoughts converse,
    And cloath them in ignoble Verse,
'Tis then I tast the most delicious Feast of Life: 25
There, uncontroul'd I can my self survey,
      And from Observers free,
    My intellectual Pow'rs display,
And all th' opening Scenes of beauteous Nature see:
Form bright Ideas, and enrich my Mind, 30
Enlarge my Knowledge, and each Error find;
Inspect each Action, ev'ry Word dissect,
And on the Failures of my Life reflect:
Then from my self, to Books, I turn my Sight,
And there, with silent Wonder and Delight, 35
Gaze on th' instructive venerable Dead,
Those that in Virtue's School were early bred,
And since by Rules of Honour always led;
Who its strict Laws with nicest Care obey'd,
And were by calm unbyass'd Reason sway'd: 40
Their great Examples elevate my Mind,
And I the force of all their Precepts find;
By them inspir'd, above dull Earth I soar,
And scorn those Trifles which I priz'd before.

3.

Next these Delights Love claims the chiefest Part, 45
That gentle Passion governs in my Heart:
Its sacred Flames dilate themselves around,
And like pure Æther no confinement know:

Where ever true Desert is found,
I pay my Love and Wonder too: 50
Wit, when alone, has Pow'r to please,
And Virtue's Charms resistless prove;
    But when they both combine,
    When both together shine,
Who coldly can behold a Glory so Divine?   55
    Since you, *Clorissa,* have a Right to these,
    And since you both possess,
You've, sure, a double title to my Love,
    And I my fate shall bless,
For giving me a Friend, in whom I find   60
United, all the Graces of the Female kind.

        4.

Accept that Heart your Merit makes your own,
And let the Kindness for the Gift attone:
Love, Constancy, and spotless Truth I bring,
These give a Value to the meanest Thing.   65
O! let our Thoughts, our Interests be but one,
Our Griefs and Joys, be to each other known:
In all Concerns we'll have an equal Share,
Enlarge each Pleasure, lessen ev'ry Care:
    Thus, of a thousand Sweets possest,   70
    We'll live in one another's Breast:
When present, talk the flying Hours away,
When absent, thus, our tender Thoughts convey;
    And, when by the Decrees of Fate
    We're summon'd to a higher State,   75
We'll meet again in the blest Realms of Light,
And in each other there eternally delight.

To Mr. *Dryden,*
on his excellent Translation of *Virgil*

            1.
Thou matchless Poet, whose capacious Mind
Contains the whole that Knowledge can impart,
    Where we each charming Science find,
        And ev'ry pleasing Art:
Permit my Muse in plain unpolish'd Verse,   5
In humble Strains her Wonder to rehearse:
From her low Shade she lifts her dazl'd Sight,
And views the Splendor and amazing Height:
See's boundless Wit, in artful Numbers play,
    And like the glorious Source of Day,   10
To distant Worlds both Light and Heat convey.

            2.
    Before the happy Birth of Light,
E'er Nature did her forming Pow'r display,
    While blended in their native Night,
        The Principles of all things lay;   15
Triumphant Darkness did her self dilate,
And thro' the Chaos with resistless Sway
        Her dusky Horrors spread;
Such in this Isle was once our wretched State:
Dark melancholy Night her sable Wings display'd,   20
And all around her baleful Influence shed;
From Gloom, to Gloom, with weary'd Steps we stray'd,
Till *Chaucer* came with his delusive Light,
And gave some transient Glimm'rings to the Night:
Next kinder *Spencer* with his Lunar Beams   25
Inrich'd our Skies, and wak'd us from our Dreams:
Then pleasing Visions did our Minds delight,
And airy Spectres danc'd before our Sight:
Amidst our Shades in antick Rounds we mov'd,
And the bright entertaining Phantoms lov'd.   30

3.

With *Waller* our first Dawn of Light arose,
He did the Beauties of the Morn disclose:
Then *Milton* came, and *Cowley* blest our Eyes;
With Joy we saw the distant Glory rise:
But there remain'd some Footsteps of the Night,　　　　35
Dark Shadows still were intermix'd with Light:
Those Shades the mighty *Dryden* chas'd away,
And shew'd the Triumphs of refulgent Day:
　　Now all is clear, and all is bright,
　　Our Sun from his Meridian height　　　　40
　　Darts kindly down reviving Rays
And one continu'd Splendor crowns our Days.

4.

This Work, great Poet, was reserv'd for thee,
None else cou'd us from our Confinement free:
By thee led on, we climb the sacred Hill,　　　　45
And our pleas'd Eyes with distant Prospects fill:
View all th' Acquests thy conqu'ring Pen has made,
　　Th' immortal Trophies of thy Fame:
And see, as if we stood on Magick Ground,
Majestick Ghosts with verdant Laurels crown'd:　　　　50
Illustrious Heroes, ev'ry glorious Name,
That can a Place in ancient Records claim:
Among the rest, thy *Virgil's* awful Shade,
Whom thou hast rais'd to bless our happy Land,
Does circl'd round with radiant Honours stand:　　　　55
He's now the welcom Native of our Isle,
And crowns our Hopes with an auspicious Smile;
With him we wander thro' the Depths below,
And into Nature's Close Recesses go;
View all the Secrets of th'infernal State,　　　　60
And search into the dark Intriegues of Fate:
Survey the Pleasures of th' *Elysian* Fields,
And see what Joys the highest Region yields.

5.

What Thanks, thou gen'rous Man, can we repay,
    What equal Retributions make,   65
    For all thy Pains, and all thy Care,
And all those Toils, whose kind Effects we share?
Our Language like th'*Augean* Stable lay,
Rude and uncleans'd, till thou by Glory mov'd,
    Th' *Herculean* Task didst undertake,   70
And hast with Floods of Wit th'offensive Heaps remov'd:
That ancient Rubbish of the *Gothick* Times,
When manly Sense was lost in trifling Rhimes:
Now th'unform'd Mass is to Perfection wrought;
Thou hast inlarg'd our Knowledge, and refin'd our Thought.   75
Long mayst thou shine within our *British* Sphere,
    And may not Age, nor Care,
The sprightly Vigor of thy Mind impair:
Let Envy cease, and all thy Merits own,
And let our due Regards in Praise be ever shown: 80
    And when from hence thou shalt remove
    To bless th'harmonious World above,
May thy strong Genius on our Isle descend,
And what it has inspir'd, eternally defend.

Song

1.

Why *Damon,* why, why, why so pressing?
The Heart you beg's not worth possessing:
Each Look, each Word, each Smile's affected,
And inward Charms are quite neglected:
    Then scorn her, scorn her, foolish Swain,   5
    And sigh no more, no more in vain.

2.

Beauty's worthless, fading, flying;
Who would for Trifles think of dying?

Who for a Face, a Shape, wou'd languish, 10
And tell the Brooks, and Groves his Anguish,
    Till she, till she thinks fit to prize him,
    And all, and all beside despise him?

3.

Fix, fix you Thoughts on what's inviting,
On what will never bear the slighting: 15
Wit and Virtue claim your Duty,
They're much more worth than Gold and Beauty:
    To them, to them, your Heart resign,
    And you'll no more, no more repine.

To *Eugenia*

Methinks I see the Golden Age agen,
Drawn to the Life by your ingenious Pen:
Then Kings were Shepherds, and with equal Care
'Twixt Men and Sheep, did their Concernments share:
There was no need of Rods and Axes then, 5
Crooks rul'd the Sheep, and Virtue rul'd the Men:
Then Laws were useless, for they knew no Sin,
From Guilt secur'd by Innocence within:
No Passion but the noblest, fill'd each Breast;
They were too good to entertain the rest: 10
Love, which is now become an Art, a Trade,
Itself to them with all its Sweets convey'd;
Indulgent Nature their kind Tutress prov'd,
And as she taught, without Deceit, they lov'd:
Thus did they live; thus they employ'd their Hours; 15
Beneath cool Shades, on Banks of fragrant Flow'rs,
They sat and listen'd, while their Poets sung
The Praises of the Brave, the Wise, the Young;
What e'er was Good, or Great, their Theme they made,
To Virtue still a Veneration paid; 20

But Love did in each Song Precedence claim,
And in soft Numbers they made known their Flame:
Poets by Nature are to Love inclin'd;
To them, the Lover's God was ever kind:
They still observ'd his Laws, and all their Care   25
Was to win Fame, and to oblige the Fair:
But ah! dear Friend, those happy Days are past;
Hard Fate! that only what is ill should last!
Unhappy we! born in the Dregs of Time,
Can ne'er to their vast height of Virtue climb;   30
But lie immers'd in Vice, forsaken quiet
Of those pure Joys which did their Souls delight:
We live disguis'd, nor can each other trust,
But only seem obliging, kind and just,
To serve our low Designs; by Int'rest sway'd,   35
That pow'rful God by all Mankind obey'd!
Nor are those Vices in the Town alone,
The Country too does with the Pressure groan:
For Innocence (once our peculiar boast)
Is now with all her Train of Virtues lost;   40
From hence to the divine Abodes retir'd
Here undeserv'd, as well as undesir'd:
Yet some imperfect Footsteps still are seen,
That future Times may know they once have been:
But oh! how few will tread that sacred way;   45
By Vice, or Humor, most are led astray:
Those few who dare be good, must live alone
To all Mankind, except themselves, unknown:
From a mad World, to some obscure Recess,
They must retire, to purchase Happiness: 50
Yet of this wretched Place so well you've writ,
That I admire your Goodness and your Wit,
And must confess your excellent Design
To make it with its native lustre shine:
To hide its Faults, and to expose to view   55
Nought but its Beauties, is becoming you.

The Wish

Would but indulgent Fortune send
To me a kind, and faithful Friend,
One who to Virtue's Laws is true,
And does her nicest Rules pursue;
One Pious, Lib'ral, Just and Brave,   5
And to his Passions not a Slave;
Who full of Honour, void of Pride,
Will freely praise, and freely chide;
But not indulge the smallest Fault,
Nor entertain one slighting Thought: 10
Who still the same will ever prove,
Will still instruct, and still will love:
In whom I safely may confide,
And with him all my Cares divide:
Who has a large capacious Mind,   15
Join'd with a Knowledge unconfin'd;
A Reason bright, a Judgment true,
A Wit both quick, and solid too:
Who can of all things talk with Ease,
And whose Converse will ever please: 20
Who charm'd with Wit, and inward Graces,
Despises Fools with tempting Faces;
And still a beauteous Mind does prize
Above the most enchanting Eyes:
I would not envy Queens their State,   25
Nor once desire a happier Fate.

The Elevation

1.
O how ambitious is my Soul,
    How high she now aspires!
There's nothing can on Earth controul,
    Or limit her Desires.

               2.
Upon the Wings of Thought she flies   5
    Above the reach of Sight,
And finds a way thro' pathless Skies
    To everlasting Light:

               3.
From whence with blameless Scorn she views
    The Follies of Mankind;   10
And smiles to see how each pursues
    Joys fleeting as the Wind.

               4.
Yonder's the little Ball of Earth,
    It lessens as I rise;
That Stage of transitory Mirth,   15
    Of lasting Miseries:

               5.
My Scorn does into Pity turn,
    And I lament the Fate
Of Souls, that still in Bodies mourn,
    For Faults which they create: 20

               6.
Souls without Spot, till Flesh they wear,
    Which their pure Substance stains:
While thy th'uneasie Burthen bear,
    They're never free from Pains.

Friendship

Friendship is a Bliss Divine,
And does with radiant Lustre shine:
But where can that blest Pair be found

That are with equal Fetters bound?
Whose Hearts are one, whose Souls combine, 5
And neither know or Mine, or Thine;
Who've but one Joy, one Grief, one Love,
And by the self same Dictates move;
Who've not a Frailty unreveal'd,
Nor yet a Thought that is conceal'd; 10
Who freely one another blame,
And strive to raise each other's Fame;
Who're always just, sincere, and kind,
By Virtue, not by Wealth, combin'd;
Whose Friendship nothing can abate, 15
Nor Poverty, nor adverse Fate,
Nor Death itself: for when above,
They'll never, never, cease to love,
But with a Passion more refin'd,
Become one pure celestial Mind. 20

The Happy Man

He is the happy Man whose constant Mind
Is to th' Enjoyment of himself confin'd:
Who has within laid up a plenteous Store,
And is so rich that he desires no more:
Whose Soul is always easie, firm, and brave, 5
And much too great to be Ambition's Slave:
Who Fortune's Frowns without Concern can bear,
And thinks it less to suffer, than to fear:
Who, still the same, keeps up his native State,
Unmov'd at all the Menaces of Fate: 10
Who all his Passions absolutely sways,
And to his Reason cheerful Homage pays,
Who's with a *Halcyon* Calmness ever blest,
With inward Joy, untroubl'd Peace, and Rest:
Who while the Most with Toil, with Guilt, and Heat, 15

Lose their dear Quiet to be Rich and Great,
Both Business, and disturbing Crouds does shun,
Pleas'd that his Work is with less Trouble done:
To whom a Grove, a Garden, or a Field,
Much greater, much sublimer Pleasures yield, 20
Than they can find in all the Charms of Pow'r,
Those splendid Ills which so much Time devour:
Who more than Life, his Friends and Books can prize,
And for those Joys the noisie world despise:
Who when Death calls, no Weakness does betray, 25
Nor to an unbecoming Fear give way;
But to himself, and to his Maxims true,
Lies smiling down, and bids Mankind adieu.

To the Ladies

Wife and Servant are the same,
But only differ in the Name:
For when that fatal Knot is ty'd,
Which nothing, nothing can divide:
When she the word *obey* has said, 5
And Man by Law supreme has made,
Then all that's kind is laid aside,
And nothing left but State and Pride:
Fierce as an Eastern Prince he grows,
And all his innate Rigor shows: 10
Then but to look, to laugh, or speak,
Will the Nuptial Contract break.
Like Mutes, she Signs alone must make,
And never any Freedom take:
But still be govern'd by a Nod, 15
And fear her Husband as her God:
Him still must serve, him still obey,
And nothing act, and nothing say,
But what her haughty Lord thinks fit,

Who with the Pow'r, has all the Wit.   20
Then shun, oh! shun that wretched State,
And all the fawning Flatt'rers hate:
Value your selves, and Men despise,
You must be proud, if you'll be wise.

To the *Queen's* most Excellent *Majesty*

        1.

MADAM,
Permit me at Your Royal Feet to lay
This humble Off'ring of a trembling Muse;
    Permit me there to pay
This Tribute to transcendent Merit due;   5
To that transcendent Merit which conspicuous is in You.
Bold is th'Address, and the Presumption high!
But she all meaner Objects does refuse,
    To this vast height will fly,
And hopes Your Goodness will th'ambitious Flight excuse.   10
I strove a while her Ardor to conceal,
    Unseen it burnt within my Breast;
But now impetuous grows, and will itself reveal;
    'Tis much too strong to be supprest.
What was at first but Warmth, now to a Flame do's rise,   15
    On you she gazes with admiring Eyes,
    And ev'ry lower Object does despise:
Pardon her Transports, since from Zeal they spring,
    And give her Leave of You to sing;
Of You, the noblest Theme that she can chuse,   20
Of You, who're with Ten thousand Graces fraught,
Of You, who far exceed the widest Bounds of Thought:
In whom as to their Centre Lines are drawn,
All those bright Qualities in one combine,
Which did till now with scatter'd Glory shine;   25
    Appear'd till now but in their Dawn:

You're the Meridian Splendor of Your Line;
And on Your Sex entail a lasting Fame:
We shall be ever proud of Your illustrious Name.

        2.

Long may You reign, long fill the *British* Throne,   30
And make the haughty *Gallick* Foe our *English* Valor own:
Assert the Rights of Your Imperial Crown;
And vie with ancient Heroes for Renown:
Tread in his Steps whom Fate has snatch'd away,
Like him the Terror of Your Arms display;   35
But longer, longer much Your happy Subjects sway,
His mighty Acts cou'd not the Victor save,
    Those Conquests he had gain'd
    Cou'd not preserve his Life:
Death to his vast Designs a Period gave,   40
Sent him amidst his Triumphs to the Grave:
For You he fought, for You he Wreaths obtain'd,
    For You he strove to humble *France:*
For You has been the Toil, for You the Strife,
    For You the Battels he has won,   45
    The wondrous things which he has done:
    To him there nothing now remains,
But empty Fame, that mean Reward for all his Pains.
Heav'n brought him here Your Grandeur to advance,
    That was the kind Design of Fate,   50
And took him hence when he had aggrandiz'd Your State.
    To You he all his Trophies yields,
To You the dusty Honours of the bloody Fields:
He at Your Feet lays all his Lawrels down.
And adds his great Atchievements to the Glories of
    Your Crown.   55

        3.

If Poets may to Prophesie pretend,
    If they're allow'd to pry,
Into the hidden Secrets of Futurity,

They dare presage, You will Your Pow'r extend,
And spite of *Salic* Laws, the *Gallick* throne ascend: 60
    For You that noble Task's assign'd,
    'Tis You are born Mankind to free,
From arbitrary Sway, and hateful Tyranny:
You, none but You, are for that Work design'd;
We no where cou'd a finer Champion find: 65
Go on great Heroin, and exalt Your Name,
Go fearless on in the bright Tracks of Fame:
When Beauty leads, and Virtue shows the Way,
The Men will soon with joyful hast obey,
None then will shew a greater Zeal than they: 70
They for Your Service with a noble Pride
    Will all Your Enemies defie,
    Will all their Vain Efforts deride,
    And strive who first for You shall die;
    Who first th' ambition'd Honour have, 75
Who first lie down in the contested Grave.

        4.
Where You reside, may Pleasures still abound,
May blooming Joys disperse themselves around,
And may there nothing there but soft Delights be found:
Still may Your Subjects make Your Bliss their Care, 80
Contending Parties in Your Cause unite:
    No more within our *British* Sphere
        May threatning Clouds appear,
        Or deafning Storms affright,
    But all be calm, and all be bright; 85
Bright as those virtues which adorn Your Mind,
Those Virtues, which we no where else can in Perfection find.
May Heav'n indulgent to Your Wishes prove,
And make You still chief Object of its Love:
Bless You with all the Favours it can give, 90
And let You in a num'rous Off-spring live;
An Off-spring worthy of Your Princely Line,
Great as Your Merit, like Your self Divine.

5.

My pious Pray'rs have quick Acceptance found,
Propitious Omens Heaven is pleas'd to send, 95
Pleas'd Nature does this glorious Change approve;
    On You she seems t'attend
    Commission'd from Above:
  Each Hour of Your auspicious Reign,
  Has been with wondrous Blessings crown'd; 100
  The Sun restores his Heat again,
  Again restores reviving Rays,
  Again we're blest with radiant Days:
  No noxious Vapors now dare rise,
  No Streams of Earth pollute the Skies, 105
Back to their gloomy Source each darkning Atom flies:
  A balmy Sweetness fills the Air,
  Health and Pleasure revel there;
  The Flow'rs rise beauteous from the Ground,
  And spread their fragrant Odors round; 110
    The Trees prepare
    Their verdant Crowns to wear;
  Amidst their Boughs soft Zephyrs play:
And in low whisp'ring Murmurs their glad Homage pay:
  The warbling Birds resound Your Praise, 115
  And welcom You with cheerful Lays:
  Joy does in every Face appear,
  In ev'ry Face is seen to smile;
  A Joy till now to us unknown,
  A Joy which You cou'd give alone; 120
  You to Your Subjects are more dear,
To us the happy Natives of this Isle,
Than Life, and all the Pleasures we possess below,
All, all the gay Delights Your *Albion* can bestow,
Which rich in You, and Your immortal Fame, 125
The Title now of Fortunate may claim,
And justly be allow'd to glory in so great a Name.

The Resolution

Yes, dear *Philistris,* in my lov'd Retreat
I will the Malice of my Stars defeat:
I've not deserv'd my Fate, and therefore dare
To brave my Fortune when 'tis most severe:
While Innocence and Honour guard my Breast,   5
I shall in spite of my worst Foes be blest:
In spite of all the Rage the Furies can inspire,
When into mortal Breasts they breath infernal Fire,
With Eyes that dart malignant Horrors round,
And Voices which affright with their tremendous Sound,   10
They fiercely may the cruel Fight begin,
And hope by Violence the Day to win;
But all in vain; I'll smiling ward each Blow,
And where my Duty calls undaunted go:
Secure within, their Shock I dare sustain,   15
My Souls impassive, and can feel no Pain:
I've secret Joys, Delights to them unknown,
In Solitude I never am alone:
Books are the best Companions I can find,
At once they please, at once instruct the Mind.   20

    Fam'd *Rochester,* who *Athens's* Plague has writ
With all the Charms of Poetry and Wit,
Does Honour on his sacred See bestow;
At once its Glory, and its Blessing too:
Him I with Pleasure read, each well weigh'd Line,   25
Delights my Soul, his Thoughts are all Divine.

    With awful Fear on *Stillingfleet* I gaze,
His wondrous Knowledge and deep Sense my ravish'd
        Soul amaze:

    Smooth *Tillotson* affords no less Delight,
None ever did with more Exactness write,   30
Or with more Clearness each dark Text unfold,

He sacred Truths intelligibly told:
Strong are his Reasons, and his Language fine,
And like his Subjects, ev'ry where Divine;

    Much the learn'd *Sarum's* pompous Stile do's please,   35
His Thoughts, tho' lofty, are express'd with Ease:
What e'er he writes so captivates the Mind,
We there the Strength of pow'rful Reason find:
See human Nature to its Zenith rais'd,
And Virtue with a winning Sweetness prais'd;   40
So charming made, and so majestick too,
We're forc'd to Love, what awfully we view:

Thou wondrous Man! who can enough admire
The amazing Force of that celestial Fire,
Which thro' each Line do's sacred Warmth inspire?   45
To darkest Minds clear dazling Light convey,
Refulgent Beams of intellectual Day!

    Th'ingenious *Norris* in a flowing Strain,
With various Scenes of Wit do's entertain;
Sometimes in Prose he sweetly do's invite,   50
And then in Verse takes an unbounded Flight:
Plato reviv'd, we in his Writings find,
His Sentiments are there, but more refin'd.
'Twould be too tedious if I all should name,
Who have a just, unquestion'd Right to Fame.   55

    O happy *Albion!* in thy Clergy blest,
In Sons that are of ev'ry Grace possest!
May they increase, and like ascending Light
Chase hence those Spectres that are pleas'd with Night,
Nor can endure a Glory so divinely bright: 60
Those restless Troublers of the Churches Peace;
May their Attacks, and their Reproaches cease;
While she supported by Almighty Love,
Securely on the wat'ry Deep do's move;

In sacred Pomp on swelling Surges rise, 65
And all the Monsters of the Main despise.

 Philosophers next these, are my Delight;
let me learn from them to think aright:
Contending Passions timely to restrain,
And o'er my self a happy Conquest gain: 70
To stand unalter'd at the Turns of Fate,
And undejected in the worst Estate.

 With Secret Pleasure I the Lives survey
Of those great Men who Virtue did obey,
And went unweary'd on in her steep painful Way; 75
Their bright Examples fortifie my Mind,
And I within both Strength and Calmness find:

 When I am wrong'd, or treated with Neglect,
I on the patient *Socrates* reflect;
That virtuous Man, who was severely try'd, 80
Who injur'd liv'd, and much more injur'd dy'd:
Methinks I see him laugh'd at on the Stage,
And made a Victim to the Poets Rage;
Expos'd, and ridicul'd, while he sits by,
And calmly bears their spiteful Calumny: 85
In him none coul'd the least Emotion find,
He bore Reproaches with a constant Mind,
And bravely met that Fate, which Fate for him design'd;
That Fate, which he persuaded was to shun;
But he resolv'd to keep the Glory he had won: 90
His Fame, to him than Life, was much more dear,
And Death was what he ne'er had learnt to fear:
Brave to the last, and to his Virtue true,
Without Concern he bid his Friends adieu,
And with a free, untroubl'd, cheerful Air, 95
Did for another, better State prepare,
And smiling drank the welcome Cure of all his Care:
That happy Draught, that Balm for all his Grief,
His best, his last, his only sure Relief.

O who wou'd live, that with such ease could go 100
From this vile World, this dismal Scene of Woe,
Where most are false, and no Compassion show,
Where our Misfortunes but a Jest are made,
Where by pretended Friends we're most betray'd:
Where Men are to their Int'rest wholly ty'd, 105
Slaves to their glitt'ring Gold, and to their Pride,
And where Ambition, and Self-love as sovereign
    Lords preside:
Where Kindness only do's to Words extend,
And few are truly that which they pretend,
And where the greatest Prodigy's a Friend. 110

Thrice happy Times when Riches were despis'd,
And Men for innate Worth were only priz'd:
When none to Titles their respect did pay,
Nor were to Bribes a mercenary Prey:
When all to rural Cares their Thoughts did bend, 115
And on their harmless Flocks with Peace attend;
When underneath some cool delightful Shade,
They to their Nymphs their artless Courtship made,
And were with kindest Vows, and unfeign'd Truth repaid:
When Constancy their highest Boast became, 120
And Friend was held the most endearing Name;
When nothing ill was harbour'd in the Mind,
But all were pious, gen'rous, just and kind.
But that blest Age, alas! was quickly past,
What's eminently good can never last: 125
Short was the peaceful *Saturn's* Golden Reign:
But oh! this Iron Age do's still remain.

Betimes the Vicious their Insults began,
And fatal was Integrity to Man:
The virtuous still to Hardships were inur'd, 130
And still the Drudgeries of Fate indur'd:
Saw Fools admir'd, and wealthy Fops carest,
And Rebels with Imperial Purple drest:

Knaves made the Props of an unthinking State,
When Truth and Justice shou'd support the Weight: 135
Ill Men ador'd, and prais'd above the Skies,
While at their Feet neglected Merit lies,
And *Regulus* amidst his Tortures dies:

   An *Aristides* from his *Athens* sent,
From his ungrateful Town to Banishment: 140

   A *Cato* bleeding in the noblest Cause,
A Victim to his Honour, and the Laws:
He reads with Pleasure of th'immortal State,
And then with hast anticipates his Fate;
With the same Courage he for *Rome* had fought, 145
He for his Soul a welcom Passage sought.

   A *Petus* strugling with a Tyrant's Rage,
A suff'ring *Arria,* Wonder of her Age!
The best of Wives, the kindest, truest Friend;
Her Spouse in all his Troubles did attend: 150
His Grief was hers, and so was all his Care;
Well pleas'd she was with him the worst of Ills to share.
When he was doom'd by his own Hand to die,
She beg'd him with the Sentence to comply;
Told him a wretched Life deserv'd no Care, 155
And that a *Roman* never ought to fear:
Bid him remember with what noble Pride
The valiant *Curtius,* and the *Decii* dy'd;
And how th'immortal *Brutus* Death's griesly Form defy'd:
But when she saw her Reasons could not move, 160
She gave a vast, a wondrous Proof of Love:
With hast she snatch'd his Poniard from his Side,
And with her dearest Blood the fatal Weapon dy'd;
Then drawing it undaunted from her Breast,
And with a Look that no Concern exprest, 165
She smiling gave it to his trembling Hand,
And said, O *Petus,* thus, thy Fate command:

Thus, *Caesar's* Malice, and thy Stars defie;
Believe me, 'tis not difficult to die.
She said no more; he sighing clos'd her Eyes,   170
And taught by her, with conscious Blushes dies;
Asham'd to think for such a noble Deed
He shou'd th' Example of a Woman need.

 An *Epictetus* in a *Nero's* Court,
The best of Men, a Slave, and Fortune's Sport.   175

 A *Belisarius,* blind, despis'd, and poor,
Seeking precarious Alms from Door, to Door;
And meanly striving to prolong his Breath,
To save a Life more to be fear'd, than Death:
While Earth-born Monsters, a degen'rous Race,   180
Rise from their Slime, and fill the heav'nly Space;
Where, for a while, like Meteors they amaze,
And fright the World with their portentous Blaze;
Till having wasted all their Stock of Light,
They fall unpity'd from their tow'ring Hight,   185
And lie despis'd in the dark Shades of Night.

 Thus *Hist'ry* Shews the World in its rude Infant State,
And does the Progress of Mankind relate;
By what slow Steps they first to Greatness rose;
Does all their Arts, their Policies disclose: 190

 There, I behold th' *Assyrian* Empire rise,
And *Babel's* lofty Tow'rs insult the Skies:
See mighty *Cyrus* all their Hopes defeat,
And place himself in the Imperial seat:
From whence I see the great *Darius* fall,   195
And the *Pellean* Youth possest of all:
Him, full of Glory, full of God-like Fire
I see amidst adoring Crouds expire:
Young *Ammon* all his boasted Conquests quit,
And early to the Laws of Fate submit: 200

He, whose Ambition towr'd above the Skies,
Now with a Spot of Earth scarce cover'd lies;
And in a dark, a narrow, silent Grave,
Sleeps undistinguish'd from his meanest Slave.

    I next observe the Western Empire rise,   205
The *Roman* Eagles wanton in the Skies:
Those Birds of *Jove* clap their extended Wings,
While with the clattering Sound the wide *Expansum* rings:
See Royal Shepherds an Usurper chase,
And on his Throne their injur'd Grandsire place;   210
With happy Omens the Foundations lay
Of that great City which the World must sway:
See *Rome's* rash Builder, the Derider kill,
And a dear Brother's Blood relentless spill.

    O what is Man, if by his Passion led!   215
Lions and Tigers with less cause we dread:
They much the gentler, much the kinder prove,
Whom nothing can against their Species move:
But Men each other's Ruin still design,
They break thro' all the Ties, the Laws Divine: 220
Nor Blood, nor Friendship, can their Rage restrain,
Intreaties all are lost, and Tears are shed in vain:
Slaves to their Will, they ev'ry Vice obey,
And on their Actions no Restriction lay.

    This fatal Truth the sad *Lucretia* found;   225
Methinks in Tears I see her almost drown'd;
Confus'd she sits among her grieving Friends,
While each to her distressful Tale attends:
Trembling and Pale, with Sighs, and downcast Eyes,
The moving Rhetorick of her Sorrow tries: 230
And then by her own Hand with wondrous Courage dies.

Pride of thy Sex! thy Glory still shall live,
To thee we will our loudest Plaudits give:

My Muse with Joy shall celebrate thy Fame,
And make the Groves resound with thy immortal Name.   235
Th' amaz'd Beholders view the breathless Fair,
And for a just, a quick Revenge prepare:
The proud *Tarquinius* with his guilty Race
They from his undeserv'd Dominions chase:
Govern'd by Consuls then, with Freedom blest,   240
And of the noblest Parts of Earth possest,
Rome long enjoy'd the Glories she had won;
But was inthrall'd at length by her victorious Son,
To his superior Fortune she gave way,
But did not long his Tyranny obey: 245
The *Roman* Soul exerts it self once more,
T'assert lost Rights, and Liberty restore;
The mighty *Caesar* to their Rage did yield,
Nor could the Goddess her lov'd Off-spring shield.
See, full of Wounds, the Hero gasping lies,   } 250
And fiercely rolling his Majestick Eyes,
Seems to call Vengeance from his Kindred Skies.

    How vain is Greatness, and how frail is Pow'r!
Those who above their Fellow Mortals tow'r,
Who with a Word can save, or with a Word destroy,   255
Can't to themselves insure one Moment's Joy:
But soon may tumble from their slippery State,
And feel the Pressures of an adverse Fate.

    Sure for our selves if we our Terms could make,
We should not Life on such Conditions take;   260
Life, which subjects us to Ten thousand Ills,
And ev'ry Minute with new Trouble fills:
By which to Fortune we're still Captives made,
And to the worst of Tyrannies betray'd;
Captives to her, who makes Mankind her Sport,   265
Who slights the best, and does the basest court;
Who low with Earth the mighty *Pompeys* lays,
And from the Dust does *Aniello's* raise.

When such Reflections, such sad Thoughts as these
On my dejected Soul begin to seize,   270
To pleasant Studies I my self apply,
And feast upon the Sweets of Poetry;
Those luscious Banquets which the Mind invite,
Where all is to be found that can delight.

Sometimes in *Homer* I the *Grecians* view,   275
See, what the King, and injur'd Husband do;
See, tow'ring *Ilium* compass'd round with Foes,
And for her sake her Sons their Lives expose;
Her valiant Sons, who prodigal of Blood,
Long in Defence of their lov'd Country stood: 280
See, from their Seats superior Pow'rs descend,
And on the *Phrygians* and the *Greeks* attend,
And with indecent warmth among themselves contend.
View fierce *Achilles* full of Grief and Rage,
Victorious *Hector* with redoubl'd Strength engage: 285
Revenge to ev'ry Blow new Force does give;
The Hopes of *Ilium* must no longer live:
Fate signs his Doom; the Godlike Hero falls,
And thrice his Body's drag'd around the *Trojan* Walls:
The *Cyprian* Goddess mourns her Favourite slain,   290
And loud Laments fill all the *Idalian* Plain.

The wise *Ulysses* does my Wonder raise,
Who can enough his prudent Conduct praise?
With his ill Fortune he did long contest,
And was not with the sight of his lov'd Princess blest: 295
The Royal Mourner for his Absence wept,
And from her Heart intruding Princes kept;
In vain they sigh'd, in vain Addresses made,
They cou'd not by their utmost Arts persuade:
To her first Vows she still did constant prove,   300
Doubly secur'd by Honour, and by Love.

The Prince of *Lyricks,* full of heav'nly Fire,
Well pleas'd I read, and as I read, admire;
Of Gods and Heroes, and of God-like Kings,
He with unequal'd Strength, and Sweetness sings: 305
Sometimes his Muse flies near, and keeps in Sight,
Then on a sudden takes a towring Flight,
And soars as high as the bright Realms of Light.
The help of mean and servile Art disdains,
While in each charming Line luxuriant Nature reigns: 310
His pregnant Fancy from its Boundless Store,
Selects the richest, and the noblest Oar,
Which his unerring Judgment so refines,
That thro' the whole a pleasing Lustre shines;
Virtue's the darling Subject of his Lays,   315
In ev'ry Ode he Piety displays,
And to the Gods due Veneration pays.
Great was the Pow'r of his immortal Song,
That could his Fame in ancient *Greece* prolong:
Twice save his House, when *Thebes* was made a Prey   320
Untouch'd that stood, while *Thebes* in Ashes lay.

    The Force of Numbers warlike *Sparta* knew,
For her what Wonders did *Tyrtæus* do!
He sung the Glories which on Fame attend;
And Honour gain'd by those who shall the State defend: 325
Who full of Courage, full of Heat Divine,
No Hazards for their Gods, and Laws, decline;
Who fear not Death, when the Reward is Praise,
That blest Exchange for all their coming Days:
The listning Soldiers with fresh Ardor fir'd;   330
As if they were by *Mars* himself inspir'd,
With furious Transports to the Field repair'd,
And met those Dangers, which before they fear'd:
Nothing *Messene* from their Rage could shield,
She to her former Lords was forc'd to yield: 335
She who to Martial Pow'r would not submit,
Was made a Prey to all-commanding Wit.

Theocritus in soft harmonious Strains,
Describes the Joys of the *Sicilian* Swains,
When with their Flocks they grace the flow'ry Plains,   340
And on their Pipes to listning Beauties play,
Who with their kind Regards the lov'd Musicians pay:
He, Nature in her native Plainness drew,
He, who the Springs of tender'st Passions knew,
Did Love in all its Infant Graces shew;   345
Love, unacquainted with deceitful Arts,
And only aiming at Exchange of Hearts.

Lucretius with his Philosophick Strains,
My Mind at once delights, and entertains:
Thro' Paths untrod, I see him fearless go;   350
His Steps I tread, with eager hast to know:
With him explore the boundless Realms of Chance,
And see the little busie Atoms dance:
See, how without Direction they combine,
And form a Universe without Design,   355
While careless Deities supremely blest,
Enjoy the Pleasures of eternal Rest,
Resolv'd that nothing here their Quiet shall molest.
Strange that a Man of such a Strength of Thought,
Could think a World was to Perfection brought   360
Without Assistance from the Pow'rs above,
From the blest Source of Wisdom, and of Love!
All frightful Thoughts he from my Soul does chase,
And in their room glad, bright Ideas place:
Tells me that Happiness in Virtue lies,   365
And bids me Death, that dreaded Ill, despise:
That Phantom, which if we but judg'd aright,
Would never once disturb, nor once affright;
The shocking Prospect of a future State,
Does in our Souls an anxious Fear create;   370
That unknown Somewhere which we must explore,
That strange, that distant, undiscover'd Shore,
Where we must land, makes us the Passage dread:

But were we by inlightned Reason led,
Were false Opinions banish'd from the Mind, 375
And we to the strict Search of Truth inclin'd,
We sure shou'd meet it with as much Delight
As the cool Pleasures of a silent Night,
And to our Graves with Cheerfulness should run,
Pleas'd that our tedious Task of Life were done. 380

   Virgil with sacred Raptures fills my Mind,
In him I unexhausted Treasures find:
While he my ravish'd Soul does entertain,
Malice and Rage employ their Shafts in vain:
Easie and pleas'd, by him I'm led along, 385
And hear the wise *Silenus's* charming Song:
Among his Nymphs and Swains with Pleasure live,
And to their Musick glad Attention give:
Then hear his Shepherds for some Prize contend,
And see his Husbandmen their much lov'd Toil attend: 390
Next with him to the burning *Ilium* go,
Where he displays Ten thousand Scenes of Woe:
Amidst the Flames the pious Prince I View,
Fearless, unmov'd, his great Designs pursue:
Like great *Alcides* he with Toil and Pain, 395
To th'utmost Height of Glory did attain,
And unrelenting *Juno's* Hate sustain;
A due Reward at length his Virtue found,
And he with Glory and with Love was crown'd.

   Horace is full of Wit, and full of Art, 400
My Mind he pleases, and inflames my Heart,
And fills my Breast with his Poetick Fire:
O that he cou'd his wondrous Heat inspire:
But mine's a pale, a languid, feeble Flame,
Wholly unworthy such a Poet's Name: 405
My humble Muse her Eyes can only raise,
Pleas'd that she has the Liberty to her Gaze,
And Leave to offer up the Tribute of her Praise.

    When by soft moving *Ovid* I am told,
Of those strange Changes which were wrought of old,   410
When Gods in Brutal Shapes did Mortals court,
And unbecoming Actions made their Sport,
When helpless Wretches fled from impious Pow'rs,
And hid themselves in Birds, Beasts, Trees, and Flow'rs:
When none from Outrage cou'd securely dwell,   415
But felt the Rage of Heav'n, of Earth, and Hell:
Methinks, I see those Passions well exprest,
Which play the Tyrant in the Mortal Breast:
They to Ten thousand Miseries expose,
And are our only, and our deadly Foes: 420
They like the Vultur on our Entrails prey,
And in our Path the Golden Apple lay,
But from us snatch our dear *Euridices* away.
Up the steep Hill the pond'rous Torment roll,
And cheat with empty Shews the famish'd Soul: 425
Those who are still submitted to their Sway,
Must in the gloomy Realms of *Pluto* stay,
And never more re-visit cheerful Day:
But those who're from their earthly Dross calcin'd,
Who tast the Pleasures of a virtuous Mind,   430
Who'd rather chuse to die, than once their Conscience stain,
Who midst Temptations Innocence retain,
And o'er themselves an undisputed Empire gain:
In th' *Elysian* Fields shall be for ever blest,
And with the Happy, there enjoy the Sweets of Rest.   435

    How well does he express unhappy Love!
Each Page does melt, and ev'ry Line does move.
The fair *Oenone* does so well complain,
That I can't chuse but blame her faithless Swain:
Good *Hypermnestra* much laments her Fate,   440
Forsaken *Phyllis* her deplor'd Estate;
Her absent Lord sad *Laodamia* mourns,
And *Sappho* for her perjur'd *Phaon* burns:
O wondrous Woman! Prodigy of Wit!

Why didst thou Man to thy fond Heart admit? 445
Man, treacherous Man, who still a Riddle proves,
And by the Dictates of his Fancy moves,
Whose Looks are Snares, and ev'ry Word a Bait,
And who's compos'd of nothing but Deceit?
What Pity 'twas thou shouldst to Love give way, 450
To Love, to vicious Love, become a Prey,
And by a guilty, inauspicious Flame,
Eclipse the Splendor of so bright a Name.

 On *Juvenal* I look with great Delight,
Both he and *Persius* with much Keeness write, } 455
They gravely teach, as well as sharply bite.

 Think not to th'ancient Bards I am alone confin'd,
They please, but never shall ingross my Mind; }
In modern Writers I can Beauties find.
Phoebus has been propitious to this Isle, 460
And on our Poets still is pleas'd to Smile.

 Milton was warm'd by his enliv'ning Fire,
Who *Denham, Waller, Cowley* did inspire, }
Roscommon too, whom the learn'd World admire: 465

 The tuneful *Dryden* felt his hottest Rays,
And long with Honour wore his freshest Bays:
The Arts, the Muses, and the Graces try
To raise his Name, and lift him to the Skie, }
And bless him with a Fame that ne'er shall die: 470
But he is gone! extinguish'd is that Light,
Which with its Lustre so long charm'd our Sight:
Yet at his Loss we dare not once repine,
While we see *Dorset* with such Glory shine,
While we see *Normanby* adorn the Skies,   475
And *Halifax* with dazling Brightness rise
That fam'd Triumvirate of Wit and Sense,
Who Laws to the whole Under-world dispence;

Whose Praise for me t'attempt, would be a Fau't,
So much are they beyond the highest flight of Thought.

    Granville the Charms of Virtue does rehearse,   480
Bright it appears in his majestick Verse:
Forsaken Honesty's his chief Delight,
To That, and Honour, he does all invite:
Commends that Peace, that Quiet of the Mind,
Which those enjoy, who to themselves confin'd   485
Forsake the noisie World, and leave its Cares behind,
Who live in Shades, where true Contentment's found,
And fly from Courts, as from unhallow'd Ground.
How wondrous good has he *Chryseis* made!
How full of Charms is that fair Captive Maid!   490
What noble Proofs of Kindness does she give!
For her *Atrides* she can wretched live!
Whom she so much above her self does prize,
That when his Safety in the Balance lies,
From his lov'd Sight, and all her Bliss she flies;   495
And rather than his Happiness destroy,
Will take an everlasting leave of Joy.
Such an Affection, such a gen'rous Flame,
Sure, the severest Censor cannot blame.
As firm, as lasting, would our Friendships prove,   500
If, as we ought, we knew but how to love:
Did Honour chuse, and Truth unite our Hearts,
If we were free from sordid wheedling Arts,
From Av'rice, Pride, and Narrowness of Mind,
We shou'd to others, as our selves be kind,   505
And all the Pleasures of a virtuous Union find.
The lov'd Commerce would more and more endear,
We with our Friends in all Concerns should share,
With them rejoice, and grieve, and hope, and fear;
And by Degrees to such an Ardor rise,   510
That we for them should Life it self despise,
And much above our own, their Satisfaction prize.

Than *Dennis* none with greater Judgment writes,
Fancy with Vigor in his Stile unites.

A Place with these, *Vanbrook* may justly claim, 515
His Thoughts are full of Wit, and full of Flame:
Instructing Sharpness runs thro' ev'ry Page;
His *Æsop's* the *Thersites* of our Age.

Than *Garth* none can with greater Smoothness write,
Just is his Stile, his Satyr is Polite: 520
Not rude like those which in the Woods are bred,
Each piercing Truth's with courtly Softness said:
But when he glorious Actions does rehearse,
And makes the Great the Subject of his Verse,
He soars aloft above the Reach of Thought, 525
And all's with wondrous Art, with wondrous Fancy wrought.
Like him, methinks, I mighty Heroes view;
See fam'd *Camillus* flying *Gauls* pursue,
The prudent *Fabius* Rome from Danger shield,
And *Carthage* to victorious *Scipio* yield: 530
The great *Nassau* unwith'ring Lawrels gain,
Unmov'd the Shock of *Gallick* Force sustain,
Fierce as the God of War on the *Phlegræan* Plain:
But he's no more: The Fair ascends Throne,
And we with Joy the lov'd *Minerva* own; } 535
Pleas'd that we Heav'ns peculiar Care are grown.

Congreve to ev'ry Theme does Beauty give,
His fair *Almeria* will for ever live.
Homer looks great in his rich *English* Dress;
So well he *Priam's* Sorrow does express, 540
That I with him for valiant *Hector* grieve;
His Suff'rings on my Mind a deep Impression leave.
With sad *Andromache* a part I bear,
With her in all her Lamentations share:
With *Hecuba* bewail a darling Son, 545
Who for his Country glorious Things had done:

His Country, which its Prop thus snatch'd away,
She knew must to the *Graecians* fall a Prey;
And she with all her House must foreign Lords obey.

    Rowe to the Skies does his great Hero raise;   550
His *Tamerlane* deserves immortal Praise:
No Pen but his cou'd ev'ry Feature trace,
No Pen but his describe each Martial Grace:
With noble Ardor to the War he goes,
And all around commanding Glances throws,   555
And fearless views Ten thousand thousand Foes:
Unwilling to destroy, he mourns their Fate,
Th'ensuing Slaughter does his Thirst of Fame abate:
When he from *Bajazet* has won the Field,
And all to his superior Virtue yield,   560
He's still the same; still humble, just, and kind;
In him we still the God-like *Scythian* find,
The same compassionate, forgiving, gen'rous Mind.

    Who for *Arpasia* can from Tears abstain?
Or hear unmov'd, her much wrong'd Prince complain?   565
With melting Softness they their Woes express;
Their Sorrows charm in his attracting Dress.
Ovid himself could not with greater Art
Describe the tender Motions of the Heart,
The Grief they feel, who must for ever part.   570

    Who beauteous *Selima* expos'd can see
To her inhuman Father's Cruelty
Without Concern? And when in such Distress
Not her *Axalla*, her Deliv'rer bless?

    May he go on, still thus adorn the Stage,   575
Still show such bright Examples to our Age,
Till he to us lost Virtue shall restore,
And we see Honour flourish here once more:
Till Justice all her ancient Rights regains,
And in her once lov'd *Albion* unmolested reigns.   580

When these have for some time employ'd my Mind, }
In other Authors I fresh Pleasures find,
And meet with various Scenes of Thoughts behind:
Lost *Montezuma* in *Accosta* view,
See what for Gold the barb'rous *Spaniards* do: 585
See the good *Inca's* bend beneath their Fate,
And dying mourn the downfal of their State:
Then with him lofty *Andes* Height ascend; }
See the fam'd *Amazon* her Streams extend,
And to the Sea her wide-stretch'd Current bend.   590

    Then view in others *Asiatick* Pride,
See a few Men the spacious East divide:
Whose hard Commands poor Wretches must obey,
Doom'd to the Mischiefs of Tyrannick Sway:
To Toil condemn'd, they pass their Time in Pain,   595
But dare not of their rig'rous Fate complain:
Nothing is theirs, their Lives are not their own,
To them no Pity, no Regard is shown:
Like Beasts they're us'd, and little more they know,
And ev'ry Place like them, does Signs of Slavery show: 600
Their Plains once fruitful, now neglected lie;
And glorious Structures which once brav'd the Skie,
Can hardly now their awful Relicks show,
We scarce can their majestick Ruins know,
While *China* govern'd by the wisest Rules,   605
And all her Nobles bred in great *Confutius* Schools,
Shews me what Art and Industry can do:
Pleas'd I their Morals and Politeness view:
Delighted see how happy they remain,
Who still the Love of Learning entertain, }   610
And where, pure uncorrupted Reason still does Reign.

    Then look on their Reverse, whom all deride,
Who seem design'd to pull down human Pride:
Those rude inhabitants of *Africk's* Shore,
Who seek no future Good, no God adore: 615
Whose Ornaments are nauseous to the Sight,

And who seem made with a Design to fright:
From such loath'd Objects I divert my Eyes,
And pity those I did at first despise,

    Why, O ye Heav'nly Pow'rs, I sighing say,   620
Are Souls condemn'd to such vile Loads of Clay,
To Bodies which their Faculties confine,
Thro' which not one celestial Ray can shine?

    We shou'd, alas! as despicable prove,
Were we not made the Care of unexhausted Love: 625
To That the diff'rence we must still assign,
And ev'ry proud aspiring Thought decline:
When we by Flatt'rers are rais'd too high,
And Man, vain Man, beyond his Sphere does fly,
Narcissus-like on's own Perfections gaze,   630
He ought to turn his Vanity to Praise,
And study to be grateful all his Days.

    While thus employ'd, I no Misfortunes fear,
And can unmov'd the greatest Troubles bear:
Quiet, and pleas'd, on my own Stock I live,   635
And to my self Content, and Riches give.

A Pindarick Ode

1.

Pleasures, like Syrens, still invite,
    And with delusive Charms,
Bewitching Baits of soft Delight,
    Allure th'unwary to their Arms:
The thoughtless Many drawn away   5
    By sweet inticing Lays,
Soon fall a voluntary Prey,
    And meanly end their Days;

  While the more manly, and the brave,
  Themselves by Resolution save:
As on the boist'rous Sea of Life they sail,
   With watchful Eyes,
  A Vigilance which ne'er can fail,
  They mark the Skies, the Rocks, the Sands:
  Still at the Helm their Reason stands,
  When she the fatal Isle descries,
  And each Inchantress sees prepare
  To tune her Voice, and lay her Snare.
She loudly cries, O my lov'd Charge, beware:
  Fly, quickly fly that dang'rous Shore;
  O see! with Bones 'tis cover'd o'er:
  Let others Ruin make you wise;
  Remote from them your Safety lies:
  They none but thoughtless Fools surprize.

    2.

  They can't to you now wing their Way,
  Their Plumes the Muses now adorn;
  They only can by Wiles betray:
  You their united Force may scorn.
  Be like the wise *Ulysses* bound,
   Pernicious freedom shun,
  Be deaf to ev'ry flatt'ring Sound;
  The most are by themselves undone:
  How few like *Orpheus* dare depend
   On their superior Skill,
  How few with good Success attend
  The fickle Motions of their Will!
  None but exalted Souls who move
By the Direction of celestial Love:
Who soar aloft, and full of heav'nly Fire,
To the Perfection of their kind aspire,
Who with Contempt view ev'ry thing below,
  And to the Source of Pleasure go,
  That pure, unmix'd, eternal Spring,

> From whence those muddy Rivers flow,
> With which we strive to quench our Thirst; 45
> To which we rav'nous Cravings bring;
> And are with wish'd Repletion curst:
> When we the largest Draughts obtain,
> We but oppressing Burthens gain;
>   Which only swell the Mind, 50
> And when they're gone, leave an uncomfortable Void behind.

3.

> Such Souls alone with Airs Divine
>   Always themselves delight:
> In vain their Skill the Tempters try,
> They both the Tempters, and their Skill defie; 55
> Their Notes are lost in Strains more bold and high,
>   Asham'd they quit their vain Design,
>   And full of anxious Spight,
>   With drooping Heads repine;
> While th' joyful Victors onward move, 60
> And chaunt the Praise of him above,
> Of him, who does their Art bestow,
> From whom harmonious Numbers flow:
> Thrice happy they who thus can live,
> Can on the mounting Billows ride, 65
> Can to themselves Contentment give,
> And void of Fear, and void of Pride,
> To lofty Heights themselves can raise,
> And sweetly warble out their Days,
> Regardless of designing, meaner Lays. 70

To the Learned and Ingenious
Dr. *Musgrave* of *Exeter*

1.

Those who like me their Gratitude would show,
    Are grieved to think they still must owe:
Be still obliged, and never know the way
The smallest part of the vast Sum to pay:
A sum beyond th' Arithmetic of Thought,   5
    And which does daily higher rise:
To be your Debtor is no more my Fault,
The whole that I can give, will not suffice:
    I am too poor Returns to make,
Unless you'll Thanks as a Requital take: 10
    Thanks are the whole that I can bring:
My Muse shall of Your wondrous Bounty sing;
Your gen'rous Temper to the World make known,
That gen'rous temper you've so often shown,
And which I still must with the highest Praises own.   15

2.

    But what, alas, is it I say!
Can I with Thanks for a loved Daughter pay?
Can her dear Life that's owing to your Care,
Any Proportion to such Trifles bear?
With weeping Eyes I saw her fainting lie,   20
        Gasping for Breath,
    But saw no Safety nigh.
As some poor Wretch who from the distant Shore,
And with insulting Waves quite cover'd o'er,
With piteous Crys does for Assistance pray,   25
    And strives t' escape the liquid Death;
Thus almost lost your helpless Patient lay,
To the devouring Waters left a Prey,
    'Till she was rescu'd by your Hand:
By such amazing Skill, and Depth of Thought,   30
Once more into the Number of the Living brought:

Where she the Trophy of your Art do's stand,
That pow'rful Art, which hitherto does save
A Life, which long since seem'd determin'd to the Grave.

3.

 Under Your Care while she remain'd,   35
 Each Day she Strength and Spirits gain'd:
 Her Health such quick Advances made,
That all with Wonder did its Progress view,
And when they look'd on her, applauded you:
But since she from your Care was snatch'd away   40
 Like Plants which want reviving Rays,
  She withers in the Shade,
   And hourly does decay:
 Had Heav'n design'd her Length of Days,
 She ne'er had been from you remov'd,   45
But Fate to her has inauspicious prov'd:
Weak as she is, she still does Thanks repay,
 Does still your former Favours own,
Those Kindnesses you've in her Sickness shown;
And in the fittest Words that she can frame,   50
She strives to pay her Homage to your Fame,
And add a worthless Mite to th' Glory of your Name.

4.

 But by a Child, and one so young,
There can be no becoming Praises sung:
 I'll undertake the Task, and try   55
 If I can her Defect supply:
My Muse shall strive to make your Virtues known;
Those virtues which you modestly conceal,
She shall to th' applauding World reveal:
Your Prudence, Truth, and Justice shall rehearse,   60
  Tho' each alone
Would prove a copious Subject for her Verse:
And you to all Mankind shall recommend,
For the sincerest, most obliging Friend,

For one in whom they may confide, on whom they
    may depend: 65
For one who's blest with all they can desire,
With whatsoever can Esteem engage;
With all those Qualities in one combin'd,
    Which singly they admire,
    And can but seldom find: 70
Who to the Coolness of delib'rate Age,
Has added all that sprightly youthful Fire,
    Which do's the noblest Thoughts inspire:
To solid Judgment, elevated Sense,
And all the Knowledge Learning can dispence, 75
Has join'd the Charms of pow'rful Eloquence.

    5.
You like a second *Æsculapius* rise,
Before you *Fame,* that noisie Goddess, flies,
And *Musgrave's* Name is echo'd thro' the Skies:
Th' obsequious Mountains answer to the Sound, 80
And friendly Winds disperse the glorious Accents round.
Diseases yield; they to your Art submit,
    And Health does on your Steps attend;
When you appear, Death must her Conquest quit;
    She dares not touch what you defend: 85
Murm'ring she flies, griev'd at her Loss of Pow'r;
And finds she must not now with so much Ease devour.
Long may you live the Blessing of this Isle,
From ev'ry Pain, and ev'ry Ill secure;
    On you may fortune ever smile, 90
    And still your Happiness ensure.
O may we long your Conversation have,
    And with the Sweets of Friendship blest,
    For num'rous Years defeat the Grave,
And keep you back from everlasting Rest; 95
Till tir'd with Length of Days, and crown'd with Fame,
You the great Privilege of Dying claim,
Pleas'd to live only here in an immortal Name.

The Observation

1.

No State of Life's from Troubles free,
Grief mixes with our vital Breath:
As soon as we begin to be,
From the first moment of our Birth,
We have some tast of Misery: 5
With Sighs and Tears our Fate we mourn,
As if our Infant Reason did presage
Th' approaching Ills of our maturer Age,
And wish'd a quick Return.
When Souls are first to their close Rooms confin'd, 10
Nothing of their Celestial Make is seen,
Obscuring Earth does interpose between:
Like Tapers hid in Urns they shine.
The Life of Sense and Growth we only see,
Which Beasts enjoy as well as we: 15
But th' active Mind
Which bears the Image of the Pow'r Divine,
Cannot exert its Energy:
The streiten'd Intellect immur'd does lie,
Shut up within a narrow place, 20
Till Nature does enlarge the Space,
And by degrees the Organs fit,
For those great Operations which are wrought by it.

2.

Thus for some Years we live by Sense,
Happy in nothing but in Innocence: 25
But when our feebler Age is past,
And we to sprightly Youth arrive,
The Race of Life we run so fast,
As if we thought our Strength would always last:
Hurry'd by Passion, and by Fancy led, 30
We all the various Paths of Folly tread:
Reason we slight, and her Commands despise,

In vain she calls, in vain advise,
And ev'ry gentle Method tries:
Against her kind Endeavours still we strive,		35
And run where ever Head-strong Passions drive:
Those Ills we court, which we as Plagues shou'd shun,
And are by ev'ry false Appearance won:
But wiser Thoughts when riper Years inspire,
We at the Follies of our Youth admire;		40
And wonder how such childish Things as these
   Cou'd Minds endu'd with Reason please;
Yet while we proudly our past Actions blame,
We do as foolish Things, tho' not the same;
Our Follies differ only in the Dress and Name.		45

		3.
Self-love so crouds the human Breast,
That there's no Room for any other Guest;
By it inspir'd we all Mankind despise,
And think our selves the only Good and Wise:
   Fond Thought! a Thought that only can		50
Become the vainest Part of the Creation, Man:
That haughty Creature, who puff'd up with Pride,
And fill'd with airy Notions soars on high,
And thinks himself the Glory of the Sky,
Where for a while in Fancy's flatt'ring Light		55
   Th'unkindl'd Vapour plays,
Much pleas'd with its imaginary Rays;
Till having wasted its small Stock of Flame,
The heavy Lump, the thing without a Name,
Falls headlong down from its exalted Height		60
Into Oblivion's everlasting Night.

Solitude

1.

Happy are they who when alone
    Can with themselves converse;
Who to their Thoughts are so familiar grown,
That with Delight in some obscure Recess,
They cou'd with silent Joy think all their Hours away,   5
And still think on, till the confining Clay
    Fall off, and nothing's left behind
Of drossy Earth, nothing to clog the Mind,
Or hinder its Ascent to those bright Forms above,
Those glorious Beings whose exalted Sense   10
Transcends the highest Flights of human Wit;
    Who with *Seraphick* Ardor fir'd,
    And with a Passion more intense
    Than Mortal Beauty e'er inspir'd;
With all th'endearing Extasies of Love,   15
Will to their blest Society again
    The long lost Wand'rers admit,
    Where freed from all their former Pain,
    And cleans'd from ev'ry Stain,
They bask with Pleasure in eternal Day,   20
And grow as pure, and as refin'd as they.

2.

But few, ah! few are for Retirement fit;
But few the Joys of Solitude can taste;
    The most with Horror fly from it,
And rather chuse in Crouds their time to waste;   25
In busie Crouds, which a Resemblance bear
    To th' unshap'd Embryo of the World,
    That formless Mass where all things were
    Without Distinction rudely hurl'd:
Tumult and Noise the Empire there had gain'd,   30
    Unrival'd there Disorder reign'd:
    The thoughtless Atoms met by chance,

Without Design they mov'd, Confusion led the Dance:
Sometimes the earthly Particles aspir'd,
    And upward forc'd their way,   35
  While the spirituous Parts retir'd,
    And near the Centre lay
Depress'd and sunk, till by the next Remove
    They disengag'd, and got above,
But cou'd not long th' impelling Shock sustain,   40
By Turns they rise, by Turns they fell again.

      3.

We in our selves a second *Chaos* find;
There is a Transcript of it in the human Mind:
Our restless Passions endless Wars maintain,
    And with loud Clamors fill the Breast: 45
Love often there the Sov'reignty does gain,
As often is by Hatred dispossess'd:
Desire the Soul with anxious Thoughts does fill,
    Insatiate boundless Thoughts instill:
      Some distant Good we view,   50
    Which we, by Hope push'd on, pursue,
Breathless, and faint, the toilsom Chase renew:
And when 'tis ours, tumultuous Joy does rise,
Ungovern'd Transport Sparkles in our Eyes;
    And we all Extasie, all Fire,   55
      The darling Prize admire,
And hug the Blessing till it does expire:
    Then to despair our selves resign,
    And sigh, and grieve, and still repine,
Curse Heav'n, our selves, our Friends, our Fate,   60
    And new, more pungent, Woes create:
    But if the Sportive Goddess lay
    A bright Temptation in our way,
    All is forgot, and full of Heat,
    Our former Toils we soon repeat;   65
    Again pursue the airy Game;
    And fond of Grandeur, Fond of Fame,

    Of Glory, Pow'r, and glitt'ring Clay,
We in laborious Nothings waste our short Remains of Day.

4.

    When distant Ills we see,   70
  The dismal Prospect us affrights,
      The sad Futurity
  Fear in our Minds excites:
And by a mean dishonourable Dread
    Of Evils which may never be,   75
  Our selves we fright, our Spirits waste,
  And often our Misfortunes haste:
  When they are present, then we rage,
  Impatient, hot, and furious grow,
  Nothing our Fury can asswage;   80
  No Limits, no Restraints we know:
  But by the Headlong Passion led,
  Without the least Demur obey;
And like some mighty Torrent force our Way:
Some mighty Torrent which no Limit knows,   85
But with a rapid Course still onward goes,
Destroys the snowy Flocks, and lays Majestick Structures low:
  But if a glimm'ring Hope arise,
  If but a Gleam of Bliss appear,
  Again we're easie, pleas'd, and gay: 90
  Forgetful of what past before,
  Above the Clouds we vainly soar:
  Impending Dangers we despise,
  And present Evils dread no more:
  And while we proudly hover there,   95
Look down with Scorn upon the Phantom Fear.

5.

Thus they alternately do lose and win,
    And all is Anarchy within:
    Reason her native Right may claim,
    And strive to re-ascend the Throne,   100

    But few, alas! her Pow'r will own:
The most to Folly their Allegiance pay,
Pleas'd with her easie, and her childish Sway:
Their Passions rule, and they contentedly obey:
Slaves to themselves they without Murmurs prove,   105
And with the meanest, worst of Servitudes in Love,
By the strong Impulse of their Vices move:
Their Chains they hug, and Wisdom's Aid refuse,
And will not her for their Director chuse:
Her Paths they shun, her Yoke they will not bear,   110
    And think her Precepts too severe:
Deaf to the Calls of Virtue and of Fame,
They madly wander thro' the Maze of Life,
Employ'd in Trifles, or engag'd in Strife:
Inslav'd by Interest, fond of glitt'ring Toys,   115
And much more pleas'd with Bubbles, than with solid Joys.

On the Death of my Honoured Mother Mrs. *Lee*: A Dialogue between *Lucinda* and *Marissa*

Lucinda. What, my *Marissa,* has *Lucinda* done,
That thus her once lov'd Company you shun?
Why is't from her you thus unkindly fly,
From her, who for your Sake cou'd freely die?
Who knows no Joy but what your Sight does give,   5
And in your Heart alone desires to live?
I beg you by that Zeal I've shewn for you,
That Tenderness which is to Friendship due,
By those dear sacred Bonds our Souls have ty'd,
Those Bonds, which Death it self shall ne'er divide;   10
By what so e'er you love, or I can name,
To let me know from whence this wond'rous
    Strangeness came.
Remember by your Vows you're wholly mine,
And I to you did all my Thoughts resign:

My Joy was yours, and yours was all my Grief, 15
In your lov'd bosom still I sought Relief:
When you were chearful, I was truly blest,
And now your Sorrow deeply wounds my Breast:
I view it thro' the thin Disguise you wear,
And spite of all your Caution, all your Care, 20
Hear ev'ry rising Sigh, and view each falling Tear.

Marissa. Permit me, dear *Lucinda,* to complain,
That your Unkindness do's augment my Pain:
How could you think that one who lov'd like me
Would ever let you share her Misery? 25
To see you mourn would bring me no Relief,
No, that would rather double all my Grief:
For Love's a Passion of the noblest kind,
And when 'tis seated in a gen'rous Mind,
'Twill be from mean Designs and Interest free 30
Not interrupt a Friend's Felicity.
Had I been happy, with a smiling Face,
I long e'er now had run to your Embrace,
And in your Arms been eager to relate
The welcom Favours of propitious Fate: 35
But since ill Fortune do's me still pursue,
O let my Griefs remain unknown to you.
Free from sad Thoughts may you for ever live,
And all your Hours to Mirth and Pleasure give:
May no Concern for me your Peace molest; 40
O let me live a Stranger to your Breast:
No more, no more my worthless Name repeat,
Abandon me to this obscure Retreat;
Make haste from hence, my Sight will damp your Joy,
And the blest Calmness of your Soul destroy. 45

Lucinda. Think not I'll leave you to your Griefs a Prey:
No! here with you I will for ever stay,
And weep with you my coming Hours away:

Return each Sigh, and ev'ry moving Groan,
And to repeating Echo's make my Moan, } 50
And tell them how unkind my lov'd *Marissa's* grown.

Marissa. To banish all Suspicions from your Mind,
And that you may not think me still unkind,
I'll let you know the Cause that makes me mourn,
The Cause that does my Joy to Sorrow turn: 55
But oh! a Loss so vast, so vastly great,
Who can without a Flood of Tears repeat!
It much too strong for my Resolves does prove,
And do's my tend' rest, softest Passions move:
Disturbs the Peace, the Quiet of my Mind, 60
And for some Minutes makes me less resign'd:
I to my Reason willingly would yield,
But strugling Nature keeps by Force the Field;
Compel'd, I stoop to her imperious Sway,
And thus each hour, methinks, I hear her say, 65
Wretched *Marissa!* all thy Comfort's fled,
And all thy Joy with thy lov'd Mother dead:
A Mother, who with ev'ry Grace was blest,
With all the Ornaments of Virtue dress'd;
With whatsoe'er Religion recommends; 70
The best of Wives, of Mothers, and of Friends.
And should not such a Loss Complaints inspire?
Their Apathy let Stoicks still admire,
And strict Obedience to their Rules require: }
And on morose, ill-natur'd, thoughtless Fools, 75
Impose the rigid Notions of their Schools:
Insensibility were here a Fault,
And 'tis a Doctrine which I never taught:
Tears are becoming, and a Tribute due
To one so worthy, and so dear to you. 80
By her thus urg'd, I gave my Sorrow way,
And did the Dictates of my Grief obey:
In this Recess, remote from Human Kind,
I thought I shou'd not Interruption find:

Most mind themselves, the Absent are forgot;   85
And this had doubtless been *Marissa's* Lot,
Had not the kind *Lucinda's* tender Care
Sought out this close Asylum of Despair,
And brought her hither all my Woes to share.

Lucinda. Such as have heard of good *Philinda's* Name,   90
Cannot with Justice sad *Marissa* blame:
A Mother's Loss, and such a Mother too,
Can't, my dear Friend, but be deplor'd by you.
All you cou'd wish she was; as Angels kind,
As Nature lib'ral, of a God-like Mind;   95
Steady as Fate, and constant in her Love;
One whom nor Wrongs, nor yet Affronts cou'd move
To mean Revenge, or a malicious Thought:
She liv'd those Truths her holy Faith had taught:
Joy cou'd not raise, nor Grief depress her Mind,   100
She still was calm, sedate, and still resign'd.

Marissa. Yes, she was more, much more than you can name,
Cheerful, obliging, gen'rous, still the same:
The Good she prais'd, the Absent did defend,
And was to the Distrest a constant Friend: 105
Full of Compassion, and from Censure free,
And of a most extensive Charity:
With winning Sweetness she did still persuade,
And her Reproofs were prudently convey'd:
In softest Language she'd the Vicious blame,   110
And none e'er lov'd with a more ardent Flame:
Her Friends Concerns she kindly made her own,
For them her greatest Care, her chief Regard was shown:
At no Misfortune she did e'er repine,
But still submitted to the Will Divine: 115
No discontented Thoughts disturb'd her Breast,
What ever happen'd, she still thought was best:
When her last Sickness came, that dire Disease
Which did on her with sudden Fury seize,

With utmost Rage the Fort of Life assail, 120
Resolv'd by racking Tortures to prevail;
O with what Patience did she bear her Pain,
And all th' Attacks of cruel Death sustain!
The dreadful Ill could not molest her Mind,
There she did still a happy Calmness find, 125
A well fixt Pleasure, a substantial Joy,
Serenity which nothing could destroy,
Sweet Antepast of what she finds above,
Where she's now blest with what she most did love;
That sov'reign Good which did her Soul inflame, 130
And whose Fruition was her utmost Aim;
And in whose Presence she do's now possess
A long desir'd, and endless Happiness.

Lucinda. Since she from all the Pains of Life is free,
And in Possession of Felicity, 135
'Tis unbecoming such a Grief to show,
As can from nothing but ungovern'd Passion flow.

Marissa. 'Tis, I confess, a Fault; but who can part
From one she loves, without a bleeding Heart?

Lucinda. 'Tis hard, I own, but yet it may be done; 140
Such glorious Victories are sometimes won:
Time will at length the greatest Grief subdue,
And shall not Reason do the same for you?
Reason, which shou'd our Actions always guide,
And o'er our Words, and o'er our Thoughts preside: 145
Passions should never that ascendant gain,
They were for Service made, and not to reign:
Yet do not think I your past Sorrow blame,
Were the Loss mine, sure, I shou'd do the same,
But having paid the Debt to Nature due, 150
No more the Dictates of my Grief pursue.
From that dark Grave where her lov'd Body lies,
Raise, my *Marissa,* your dejected Eyes,
And view her Soul ascending to the Skies,

By Angels guarded, who in charming Lays,   155
Sing as they mount, their great Creator's Praise;
And to celestial Seats their Charge convey,
To never ending Bliss, and never ending Day:
And is't not cruel, or at least unkind
To wish that she were still to Earth confin'd,   160
Still forc'd to bend beneath her Load of Clay?
Methinks I hear the glorious Vision say,
What is't, *Marissa,* makes you still complain,
Are you concern'd that I am void of Pain,
And wou'd you have me wretched once again?   165
Have me t'exchange this Bliss for Toil and Fear,
And all these Glories for a Life of Care?
Or is't th'Effect of a too fond Desire,
Do's Love, mistaken Love, these Thoughts inspire?
Is it my Absence you so much deplore,   170
And do you grieve because I'm yours no more,
Because with me you can no more Converse,
No more repeat your wrongs, or tell me your distress,
No more by my Advice your Actions steer,
And never more my kind Instructions hear?   175
If this do's cause your Grief, no more Complain;
'Twill not be long e'er we shall meet again;
Shall meet all Joy in these bright Realms of Love,
And never more the Pains of Absence prove:
Till that blest Time, with decent Calmness wait,   180
And bear unmov'd the Pressures of your Fate.

Marissa. Yes, my dear Friend, I your Advice will take,
Dry up my Tears, and these lov'd Shades forsake:
I can't resist, when Kindness leads the Way;
I'm wholly yours, and must your Call obey: 185
With you to hated Crouds and Noise I'll go,
And the best Proofs of my Affection show:
But where soe'er I am, my troubl'd Mind
Will still to my *Philinda* be confin'd;
Her Image is upon my Soul imprest,   190

She lives within, and governs in my Breast:
I'll strive to live those Virtues she has taught,
They shall employ my Pen, my Tongue, my Thought:
Where e'er I go her Name my Theme shall prove,
And what soe'er I say, shall loudly speak my Love.   195

On the Death of my dear Daughter
Eliza Maria Chudleigh:

A Dialogue between *Lucinda* and *Marissa*

Marissa. O my *Lucinda!* O my dearest Friend!
Must my Afflictions never, never End!
Has Heav'n for me no Pity left in Store,
Must I! O must I ne'er be happy more,
Philinda's Loss had almost broke my Heart,   5
From her, Alas! I did but lately part:
And must there still be new Occasions found
To try my Patience, and my Soul to wound?
Must my lov'd Daughter too be snatch'd away,
Must she so soon the Call of Fate obey?   10
In her first Dawn, replete with youthful Charms,
She's fled, she's fled from my deserted Arms.
Long did she struggle, long the War maintain,
But all th'Efforts of Life, alas! were vain.
Could Art have sav'd her she had still been mine,   15
Both Art and Care together did combine,
But what is Proof against the Will Divine!
    Methinks I still her dying Conflict view,
And the sad Sight does all my Grief renew:
Rack'd by Convulsive Pains she meekly lies,   20
And gazes on me with imploring Eyes,
With Eyes which beg Relief, but all in vain,
I see, but cannot, cannot ease her Pain:
She must the Burthen unassisted bear,

I cannot with her in her Tortures share: 25
Wou'd they were mine, and she stood easie by;
For what one loves, sure 'twere not hard to die.
    See, how she labours, how she pants for Breath,
She's lovely still, she's sweet, she's sweet in Death!
Pale as she is, she beauteous does remain, 30
Her closing Eyes their Lustre still retain:
Like setting Suns, with undiminish'd Light,
They hide themselves within the Verge of Night.
    She's gone! she's gone! she sigh'd her Soul away!
And can I! can I any longer stay! 35
My Life, alas! has ever tiresome been,
And I few happy, easie Days have seen;
But now it does a greater Burthen grow,
I'll throw it off and no more Sorrow know,
But with her to calm peaceful Regions go. 40
    Stay thou, dear Innocence, retard thy Flight,
O stop thy Journy to the Realms of Light,
Stay till I come: To thee I'll swiftly move,
Attracted by the strongest Passion, Love.

Lucinda. No more, no more let me such Language hear, 45
I can't, I can't the piercing Accents bear:
Each Word you utter stabs me to the Heart:
I cou'd from Life, not from *Marissa* part:
And were your Tenderness as great as mine,
While I were left, you would not thus repine. 50
My Friends are Riches, Health, and all to me,
And while they're mine, I cannot wretched be.

Marissa. If I on you cou'd Happiness bestow,
I still the Toils of Life wou'd undergo,
Wou'd still contentedly my Lot sustain, 55
And never more of my hard Fate complain:
But since my Life to you will useless prove,
O let me hasten to the Joys above:
Farewel, farewel, take, take my last adieu,

May Heav'n be more propitious still to you 60
May you live happy when I'm in my Grave,
And no Misfortunes, no Afflictions have:
If to sad Objects you'll some Pity lend,
And give a Sigh to an unhappy Friend,
Think of *Marissa,* and her wretched State, 65
How she's been us'd by her malicious Fate,
Recount those Storms which she has long sustain'd,
And then rejoice that she the Port has gain'd,
The welcome Haven of eternal Rest,
Where she shall be for ever, ever blest; 70
And in her Mother's, and her Daughter's Arms,
Shall meet with new, with unexperienc'd Charms.
O how I long those dear Delights to taste;
Farewel, farewel; my Soul is much in haste.
Come Death and give the kind releasing Blow; 75
I'm tir'd with Life, and over-charg'd with Woe:
In thy cool, silent, unmolested Shade,
O let me be by their dear Relicks laid;
And there with them from all my Troubles free,
Enjoy the Blessings of a long Tranquillity. 80

Lucinda. O thou dear Suff'rer, on my Breast recline
Thy drooping Head, and mix thy Tears with mine:
Here rest a while, and make a Truce with Grief,
Consider; Sorrow brings you no Relief.
In the great Play of Life we must not chuse, 85
Nor yet the meanest Character refuse
Like Soldiers we our Gen'ral must obey,
Must stand our Ground, and not to Fear give way,
But go undaunted on till we have won the Day.
Honour is ever the Reward of Pain, 90
A lazy Virtue no Applause will gain,
All such as to uncommon Heights would rise,
And on the Wings of Fame ascend the Skies,
Must learn the Gifts of Fortune to despise.
They to themselves their Bliss must still confine, 95

Must be unmov'd, and never once repine:
But few to this Perfection can attain,
Our Passions often will th'Ascendant gain,
And Reason but alternately does reign;
Disguis'd by Pride, we sometimes seem to bear
A haughty Port, and scorn to shed a Tear;
While Grief within still acts a tragick Part,
And plays the Tyrant in the bleeding Heart.
Your Sorrow is of the severest kind,
And can't be wholly to your Soul confin'd:
Losses like yours, may be allow'd to move
A gen'rous Mind, that knows what 'tis to love.
Who that her innate Worth had understood,
Wou'd not lament a Mother so divinely good?
And who, alas! without a Flood of Tears,
Cou'd lose a Daughter in her blooming Years:
An only Daughter, such a Daughter too,
As did deserve to be belov'd by you;
Who'd all that cou'd her to the World commend,
A Wit that did her tender Age transcend,
Inviting Sweetness, and a sprightly Air,
Looks that had something pleasingly severe,
The Serious and the Gay were mingl'd there:
These merit all the Tears that you have shed,
And could Complaints recall them from the Dead,
Could Sorrow their dear Lives again restore,
I here with you for ever would deplore:
But since th'intensest Grief will prove in vain,
And these lost Blessings can't be yours again,
Recal your wand'ring Reason to your Aid,
And hear it calmly when it does persuade;
'Twill teach you Patience, and the useful Skill
To rule your Passions, and command your Will;
To bear Afflictions with a steady Mind,
Still to be easie, pleas'd, and still resign'd,
And look as if you did no inward Trouble find.

Marissa. I know, *Lucinda,* this I ought to do,
But oh! 'tis hard my Frailties to subdue:
My Head-strong Passions will Resistance make,
And all my firmest Resolutions shake: 135
I for my Daughter's Death did long prepare,
And hop'd I shou'd the Stroke with Temper bear,
But when it came, Grief quickly did prevail,
And I soon found my boasted Courage fail:
Yet still I strove, but 'twas, alas! in vain, 140
My Sorrow did at length th'Ascendant gain:
But I'm resolv'd I will no longer yield;
By Reason led, I'll once more take the Field,
And there from my insulting Passions try
To gain a full, a glorious Victory: 145
Which till I've done, I never will give o'er,
But still fight on, and think of Peace no more;
With an unweary'd Courage still contend,
Till Death, or Conquest, does my Labour end.

The Offering

1.

Accept, my God, the Praises which I bring,
The humble Tribute from a Creature due:
   Permit me of thy Pow'r to sing,
That Pow'r which did stupendous Wonders do,
And whose Effects we still with awful Rev'rence view: 5
That mighty Pow'r which from thy boundless Store,
   Out of thy self where all things lay,
   This beauteous Universe did call,
This Great, this Glorious, this amazing All!
And fill'd with Matter that vast empty Space, 10
   Where nothing all alone
Had long unrival'd sat on its triumphant Throne.
   See! now in every place

   The restless Atoms play:
  Lo! high as Heav'n they proudly soar,   15
   And fill the wide-stretch'd Regions there;
In Suns they shine Above, in Gems Below,
And roll in solid Masses thro' the yielding Air:
In Earth compacted, and diffus'd in Seas;
In Corn they nourish, and in Flow'rs they please: 20
   In Beasts they walk, in Birds they fly,
And in gay painted Insects croud the Skie:
In Fish amid the Silver Waves they stray,
And ev'ry where the Laws of their first Cause obey:
  Of them, compos'd with wondrous Art,   25
   We are our selves a part:
And on us still they Nutriment bestow;
To us they kindly come, from us they swiftly go,
And thro' our Veins in Purple Torrents flow.
   Vacuity is no where found,   30
Each Place is full: with bodies we're encompass'd round:
   In Sounds they're to our Ears convey'd,
In fragrant Odors they our Smell delight,
And in Ten thousand curious Forms display'd,
   They entertain our Sight: 35
   In luscious Fruits our Tast they court,
And in cool balmy Breezes round us sport,
The friendly Zephyrs fan our vital Flame,
And give us Breath to praise his holy Name,
From whom our selves, and all these Blessings came.   40

    2.
Receive my Thanks, 'tis all that I can pay,
The whole I can for num'rous Favours give;
   Their Number does increase each Day,
I still on unexhausted Bounty live:
My Life, my Health, the Calmness of my Mind,   45
All those Delights I in my Reason find,
Those dear Delights which are from all the Dregs of
   Sense refin'd,

Are Donatives of Love Divine,
The Benefactor in his Gifts does shine:
His boundless Goodness still it self displays,
Still warms with kind refulgent Rays:
   In it the whole Creation share;
   The whole Creation is his Care:
   All Beings upon him depend;
To whatsoe'er he made, still his Regards extend:
   Nothing's so high, nor yet so low,
      As to escape his Sight,
He do's the Wants of all his Creatures know,
And to relieve them is his chief Delight,
A Pleasure worthy that Almighty Mind,
Whose Kindness like himself is unconfin'd.

        3.
Ah! thankless Mortals, can't such wondrous Love,
   Inspire you with a grateful Sense?
   Can't such amazing Favours move?
Must he his Blessings unobserv'd dispence,
   Have no Return, no Tribute paid,
No Retributions for such Bounties made?
O think, and blushing at his Footstool fall,
   There beg his Pardon, prostrate lie,
And for Forgiveness to his Mercy fly:
Remember 'tis to him you owe your All,
He gives you Pow'r upon himself to call:
Should he from you his Aid withdraw,
   You quickly wou'd have cause to mourn,
   And sighing to your Dust return:
He is your Strength, your Life, your Light,
He to your jarring Principles gives Law,
   And the Destroyer Death does awe:
   His Angels compass you around,
And keep off Ills from the forbidden Ground:
By his Command you're ever in their Sight,
And made at once their Care, and their Delight:

O quickly then your Gratitude express,
And as becomes you, your Creator bless:
Before his Throne melodious Off'rings lay, 85
And in harmonious Strains your long neglected
      Homage pay.

      4.

I'll strive with you my Zeal to show,
    With you I'll strive to pay
Some little Part of what I owe:
My self before his Throne I'll lay, 90
My self, and all he does on me bestow:
    My Reason for him I'll employ,
    And in his Favour place my Joy:
    His Favour which to me's more dear
    Than all the tempting Glories here: 95
My Tongue shall still extol his Name,
    Shall still his wondrous Works proclaim:
My Mem'ry shall his Kindnesses inrol,
    And fix them firmly in my Soul:
    From him my Thoughts no more shall stray, 100
    No more my Passions I'll obey,
No more to the rash Dictates of my Will give Way,
But still to him, and him alone, a glad Submission pay.

      5.

    To Love I will my self resign;
    But it shall be to Love Divine: 105
    That o'er me ever shall preside,
Shall ev'ry Word, and ev'ry Action guide:
    To it I will my self unite,
    In it I'll place my sole Delight,
    And ev'ry meaner Object slight; 110
    Till one at last with it I grow,
And tir'd with treading this dull Round below,
To its blest Source with eager Swiftness go;
To its blest Source, where constant Joys are found,

And where ne'er ending Pleasures spread themselves
  around;   115
Where nothing's wanting that we can desire,
Where we to nothing greater can aspire,
And where e'en Thought it self can soar to nothing higher.

The Resolve

1.

For what the World admires I'll wish no more,
 Nor court that airy nothing of a Name:
Such flitting Shadows let the Proud adore,
 Let them be Suppliants for an empty Fame.

2.

If Reason rules within, and keeps the Throne,   5
 While the inferior Faculties obey,
And all her Laws without Reluctance own,
 Accounting none more fit, more just than they.

3.

If Virtue my free Soul unsully'd keeps,
 Exempting it from Passion and from Stain: 10
If no black guilty Thoughts disturb my Sleeps,
 And no past Crimes my vext Remembrance pain.

4.

If, tho' I Pleasure find in living here,
 I yet can look on Death without Surprize:
If I've a Soul above the Reach of Fear,   15
 And which will nothing mean or sordid prize.

5.

A Soul, which cannot be depress'd by Grief,
 Nor too much rais'd by the sublimest Joy;

Which can, when troubled, give it self Relief,
    And to Advantage all its Thoughts employ.   20

        6.
Then am I happy in my humble State,
   Altho' not crown'd with Glory nor with Bays:
A Mind, that triumphs over Vice and Fate,
   Esteems it mean to court the World for Praise.

One of *Lucian's* Dialogues of the Dead Paraphras'd

Diogenes. O *Pollux,* when thou next revisit'st Light,
Menippus to these nether Realms invite;
Tell him, if he's not tir'd with Fools above,
Where all that's said, and done, his Mirth does move,
He'll here fit Subjects for his Laughter find,   5
New Scenes of Madness to divert his Mind:
For tho' blind Mortals no Ideas have
Of any thing beyond the silent Grave,
But vainly fancy, as their Toil and Care,
So too their Souls find equal Periods there,   10
And all the dislodg'd Atoms mingle with the Air.
Yet here are no such impious Scepticks found,
Each Place does with complaining Ghosts abound:
He sure with me would full of Wonder gaze
On mighty Men whose glorious Acts amaze,   15
Who conquer'd Kingdoms, and who Thrones did grace,
And left their Sceptres to their God-like Race,
Here, undistinguish'd from the meanest Shade,
Depriv'd of Grandeur, and by none obey'd:
They by no other marks can now be known,   20
But Sighs, and Groans, and sad Complaints alone:
But bid him with him some Provisions bring,
A Crust were here a Present for a King:
He'll here find nothing Nature to sustain,
Throughout the vast Extent of this dark empty Plain.   25

Pollux. I'll readily perform what you desire;
But tell me where I shall for him inquire;
Describe his Person, Humor, and Attire.

Diogenes. He's old and jolly, and to *Bacchus* kind,
To Fools averse, to Satire still inclin'd: 30
A Cloak he wears the poorest Wretch wou'd scorn,
And which Ten thousand Patches wretchedly adorn:
At *Athens,* or at *Corinth* him you'll find,
Lampooning the whole Race of Human Kind:
He strikes at all, both th' Ugly and the Fair,   35
Nor Young, nor Old, nor yet the Great does spare,
But on Philosophers is most severe:
Their vain Pretences, and their towring Flights,
Their mystick Terms, and all those little Slights,
By which they strive their Ignorance to hide,   40
Those Cobweb Cov'rings for their nauseous Pride,
Are still the Subjects which his Laughter move
The chief Diversion that he finds above.

Pollux. By this Description he'll with ease be known:
But is your Message sent to him alone?   45
Can you not think of something that is fit
To be deliver'd to those Men of Wit,
Those high Pretenders to gigantick Sense,
To boundless Knowledge, matchless Eloquence?

Diogenes. Bid them lay all their vain Disputes aside,   50
No longer Truth from their Disciples hide:
No more thro' Nature's puzling Labyrinths stray,
No more of her mysterious Motions say:
No more with an affected haughty Air,
Their Thoughts of Things beyond their reach declare,   55
Things far remote from the most piercing Sight,
Beyond the Ken of intellectual Light.

Pollux. Such a Discourse as this wou'd not be born,
'Twou'd both expose me to their Hate, and Scorn:
They'll gravely tell me, I my Ign'rance show,   60
And rail at what I want the Sense to know.

Diogenes. Tell them from me th'important Message came;
'Tis I their Pride and Ignorance proclaim:
I bid them with Remorse past Follies view,
And their Repentance by their Blushes shew.   65

Pollux. I with exactest Care your Order will obey,
Without being mov'd at what the noisie Boasters say.

Diogenes. When this is done, then to the Great repair,
And speak to them with a commanding Air:
Say, What ye mad Men, makes you thus in vain,   70
To heap up Honours, and increase your Train,
As if you here for ever shou'd remain?
Riches and Grandeur do but load the Mind,
And they are Trifles you must leave behind:
Naked and poor, you to the Shades must go,   75
Only Despair will stay with you below:
The more you've now, the more you will lament,
When you from all your Pomp, and all your Joys are sent.
Next to th'Effeminate *Megilbus* go,
And let the brawny *Damoxenus* know   80
That none below are handsom, strong, or brave;
All are meer Phantoms when they're past the Grave:
None here their Youth and boasted Charms retain,
None here the fam'd *Olympick* Prizes gain:
No killing Eyes bewitching Glances dart,   85
No flowing Tresses win an amorous Heart:
No blushing Cheeks, not one inticing Smile,
Can here be seen th'unwary to beguile:
Nothing is lovely, nothing pleasing here,
Nothing but Dust and Ashes does appear.   90

Pollux. This I with Speed, and with Delight will do,
Since 'tis a Message worthy me, and you.

Diogenes. Inform the Poor, of whom vast Crouds you'll see,
That here they'll find a just Equality;
Tell' em, they'll here unhappy Partners find,   95
Afflictions are not to one State confin'd:
Millions of Suff'rers throng the *Stygian* shore,
And there for ever will their Fate deplore,
Then bid them to complain and weep no more;
Since none will here their former Pomp retain,   100
But on a humble Level all remain:
None here will richer, greater, happier live,
No flatt'ring Tides to each other give:
No Room is left for Av'rice, or for Pride,
Where Poverty and Death, and dreadful Night reside.   105
And then from me, degen'rate *Sparta* blame,
Tell them they've tarnish'd their once glorious Fame;
They now no longer breath that Martial Heat,
Which made them once so formidably Great.

Pollux. Such Words as these, *Diogenes,* forbear,   110
I can't with Patience such Reproaches hear:
My Country's Honour, as my own, I prize,
And cou'd for it my Share of Life despise.
All your Commands, but this, without Delay
I'll e'er to morrow Night with Care obey.   115

Diogenes. 'Tis kindly said; I will no more desire:
May *Hermes* his persuasive Skill inspire,
And may your Voice be sweet as th'*Orphean* Lyre
That list'ning Mortals, by your Precepts taught,
May to the Knowledge of their Faults be brought,   120
Reclaim'd from Ill, and made themselves to know:
A Lesson they too late will learn below!

To the *Queen's* most Excellent *Majesty*

  When Heav'n designs some wondrous Prince to raise,
Deserving Empire and eternal Praise;
It chuses one of an illustrious Line,
In whom Hereditary Graces shine:
Who good and great by his Descent is made,   5
And by the Rules of native Honour sway'd:
Him it exposes to th' Insults of Fate,
To all the Blows of Malice and of Hate,
Before it raises him to an exalted State.

  The pious *Trojan,* its peculiar Care,   10
Did num'rous Hardships, num'rous Trials bear;
Ten thousand Toils with Patience he sustain'd,
Before he undisturb'd in *Latium* reign'd:
To pains inur'd, with Disappointments crost,
Wan'dring thro' Flames, on mounting Surges tost: 15
Suff'rings and War to Grandeur led the Way,
And fitted him for independent Sway.

  Happy that People whose blest Monarch owes
Unto himself the Wisdom which he shows,
Whose Prudence from his own Experience flows.   20
Who has in Shades seen dark'ning Vapors rise,
And gloomy Horrors over' cast the Skies:
Neglected liv'd in some obscure Retreat,
And learnt in secret to be truly great;
To rule within, his Passions to subdue,   25
And all his Souls most hidden Movements view:
Those Springs of Thought, which when they are refin'd
Bestow a dazling Brightness on the Mind:
Who disengag'd from Bus'ness and from Noise,
To noblest Purposes his Hours employs: 30
Searches past Records, and with vast Delight
Presents fam'd Heroes to his ravish'd Sight:
Sees them the shining Paths of Honour tread,

By Praise push'd on, and daring Courage led:
With eag'rest Hast to lofty Heights ascend,   35
And their Renown beyond the Grave extend:
Sees pious Kings with Joy and Zeal obey'd,
And cheerful Homage to wise Princes paid:
Who're still the Objects of a filial Love,
Whom all admire, whose Actions all approve.   40

    Such was that Virgin Glory of our Isle,
On whom *Apollo* long was pleas'd to smile:
Who was with Wisdom and with Science bless'd,
By ev'ry Muse, and ev'ry Grace caress'd:
She knew Afflictions, felt a Sister's Hate,   45
And learnt to reign, while in a private State;
By adverse Fortune taught her self to know,
That Knowledge chiefly requisite below.

    And such the Queen who now the Throne does grace,
The brightest Glory of her Royal Race: 50
In whose rich Veins the noblest Blood does flow
That God-like Kings, and Heroes could bestow:
Like her she bravely stood the Shock of Fate,
And liv'd serene in a dependent State:
Bore unconcern'd the Calumnies of those   55
Whom their Ill-nature only made her Foes:
Who thought her Merit too divinely bright,
And move t'eclipse the overflowing Light:
Merit in narrow Minds does Envy raise,
Large gen'rous Souls are most inclin'd to Praise.   60
Like her she stem'd the dang'rous swelling Tide,
And soar'd aloft with a becoming Pride:
Like her a gen'ral Approbation found,
And was with joyful Acclamations crown'd:
Ev'n Heav'n it self her Unction did approve,   65
And by auspicious Omens shew'd its Love:
Refreshing Breezes fan'd the balmy Air,
The fertile Earth a florid Green did wear:

No Clouds obscur'd the Sun's refulgent Light,
He never shone more eminently bright: 70
All things conspir'd her Welcom to proclaim,
Who the Protectress of her People came,
By Heav'n design'd, and her propitious Fate,
To be the Bulwark of a tott'ring State.

   Britannia now all glorious does arise, 75
And shoots her Head above the starry Skies:
Her sacred Guardian, all the Sons of Light,
With Shouts of Joy behold the pleasing Sight:
The list'ning Goddess hears the cheerful Sound,
From Hill to Hill, from Vale to Vale rebound: 80
On all her Plumes at once, sublime she flies,
At once employs her num'rous Tongues and Eyes:
To distant Lands our Happiness makes known;
Tells them a Heroin fills the *British* Throne:
A Heroin greater than Romance can frame, 85
And worthy of the Line from whence she came;
In whom the Great and Brave, the Soft and Kind,
In One are by the firmest Ties combin'd:
Where nothing's wanting that we can desire,
And where we see each Minute something to admire. 90

   The trembling Nations aw'd by *Gallick* Arms,
Imploring come, drawn by resistless Charms:
To her they sue, and beg from her Relief;
She looks with God-like Pity on their Grief:
Exerts her Pow'r, and makes th' *Iberian* Shore; 95
The *Spaniards* hear her murth'ring Canon roar?
Her Fleet dilates a panick Terror round,
And *British* Valor's once more dreadful found:
Her Troops descend with noble Ardor fir'd,
By Heav'n, and their Heroick Queen inspir'd: 100
In vain they strive their darling Gold to save,
What can resist the Daring and the Brave?
Those Sons of War thro' Dangers force their Way,

And from the Dragons snatch the shining Prey:
Fame spreads the News thro' all th'incircling Air;   105
Aloud proclaims the Triumphs of the Fair:
The drooping Eagles prune their Wings and rise,
With joyful Haste they cut the sounding Skies;
Secure once more of that auspicious Fate
Which on them did so many Ages wait: 110
The *Belgick* Lion casts his Fear away,
And with new Strength pursues the destin'd Prey:
All the Distrest with Raptures of Delight,
In sweetest Songs of grateful Praise unite:
Blest *Albion's* Queen their only Theme does prove;   115
Like *Pallas* sprung from all-commanding *Jove*,
She comes, they sing, to give us timely Aid,
Is kind, and wise, as that celestial Maid:
As able to advise, and to defend,
And does her Care to ev'ry Part extend: 120
Like *Phoebus* darts reviving Beams of Light,
And dissipates the Horrors of the Night.

    O that I cou'd the best of Queens attend;
Cou'd at your Feet my coming Moments end:
I past Misfortunes shou'd not then deplore,   125
And present Evils wou'd afflict no more:
But fill'd with Joy, with Transport, and with Love,
My Hours wou'd in a blissful Circle move:
And I the noblest Bus'ness still wou'd chuse,
Both for my self, and my ambitious Muse,   130
Be still employ'd in Service, and in Praise,
In glad Attendance, and in grateful Lays.

from Song of the Three Children Paraphras'd

22.

By Heat excited, Exhalations rose,
And did the Regions of the Air compose:
The thicker Parts our Atmosphere did frame,   490
While the more subtil took a nobler Flight,
And fill'd with purest *Æther* the celestial Height,
Then Land appear'd; th' obsequious Floods gave way,
And each within appointed Bounds did stay;
But rude and unadorn'd the new Concretion lay,   495
Till by a sudden Act of Pow'r Divine,
Th' unshap'd Mass a beauteous Earth became;
Charming it look'd in its gay Infant Dress;
    Goodness and Art at once did shine,
        And both the God confess.   500
Thrice blest that Pair, who in the Dawn of Time
Were made Possessors of that happy Clime:
But wretched they soon lost their blissful State,
Undone by their own Folly, not their Fate.

23.

Serene and Calm those early Regions were,   505
    A constant Spring was always there,
    And gentle Breezes cool'd the Air,
    Rough Winds and Rains they never knew,
    But unseen Showr's of pearly Dew,
(Aereal Streams) their Balmy Drops distill'd,   510
And with prolifick moisture the smooth surface fill'd.
The beauteous Plains perpetual Verdure wore,
    With lovely Flow'rs embroider'd o'er.
Flowers so wondrous sweet, so wondrous Fair,
Ne'er grac'd our Earth, never perfum'd our Air,   515
Peculiar to those happier Fields they were;
Thro' which the winding Rivers make their Way,
The clear unsullied Streams with wanton Play
    In Thousand various Figures Stray;
    Sometimes concurring Waters make   520

    A little Sea, a Chrystal Lake,
Where for a while in their soft Bed they rest,
    Till by succeeding Currents prest,
    To distant Parts they gently flow,
        And murmur as they go,   525
    As if they wish'd a longer Stay,
    And ran unwillingly away:
    On their enamel'd banks were seen
    Plants ever Beauteous, ever Green;
    Plants, whose odoriferous Smell,   530
Did the since fam'd *Sabæan* sweets excell.
Nature profusely spread her Riches there,
The fertile Soil prov'd grateful to her Care,
The new unlabour'd Ground large stately Trees did bear,
Trees whose Majestick Tops aspir'd so high,   535
They almost seem'd to touch the Sky;
Loaden with Blossoms, and with Fruit at once they stood;
At once the Beauties of the Spring and Autumn crown'd
    the Wood:
At once they did the Bounties of both Seasons wear.

24.

Such was the Earth so Beauteous and so Gay,   540
Fresh as the Morn, delightful as the Day:
Not the *Hesperian* Gardens so much fam'd of old,
Where glorious Trees bare vegetable Gold;
Nor that whereof *Mæonides* has writ,
Alcinous Garden, which its Beauty ow'd   545
To that great Genius, that transcendent Wit,
    Who could the lowest Subject raise,
And make the meanest things deserve Eternal Praise:
Such was *Phæacia,* 'till with wondrous Art
    He 'mbelish'd ev'ry Part: 550
    His Fancy the rich Dress bestow'd:
To future Times it had been little known,
Having no native Lustre of its own,
    Had not his Muse enroll'd its Name,

And laid it up secure within th' Archives of Fame. 555
    Nor these, nor yet those happy Plains,
Virgil describes in his immortal Strains,
Could equal the Perfections of that charming Place,
Which Nature had adorn'd with her exactest Care,
    And furnish'd it with every Grace; 560
    Her Skill did every where appear:
All that was lovely, all that lov'd Delight,
Might there be seen in its exalted Height:
    In it conspicuously did shine
Th' inimitable Strokes of Art Divine, 565
The God was seen in every dazling Line.

from **The Ladies Defence**

Melissa. I've still rever'd your Order as Divine;
And when I see unblemish'd Vertue Shine,
When solid Learning, and substantial Sense,   490
Are joyn'd with unaffected Eloquence;
When Lives and Doctrines of a Piece are made,
And holy Truths with humble Zeal convey'd;
When free from Passion, Bigottry and Pride,
Not sway'd by Interest, nor to Parties ty'd,   495
Contemning Riches, and abhorring Strife,
And shunning all the noisie Pomps of Life,
You live the aweful Wonders of your Time,
Without the least suspicion of a Crime:
I shall with Joy the highest Deference pay,   500
And heedfully attend to all you say.
From such, Reproofs shall always welcome prove,
As being th' Effects of Piety and Love.
But those from me can challenge no Respect,
Who on us all without just Cause reflect: 505
Who without Mercy all the Sex decry,
And into open Defamations fly:
Who think us Creatures for Derision made,
And the Creator with his Work upbraid:
What he call'd Good, they proudly think not so,   510
And with their Malice, their Prophaneness show.
'Tis hard we should be by the Men despis'd,
Yet kept from knowing what wou'd make us priz'd:
Debarr'd from Knowledge, banish'd from the Schools,
And with the utmost Industry bred Fools.   515
Laugh'd out of Reason, jested out of Sense,
And nothing left but Native Innocence:
Then told we are incapable of Wit,
And only for the meanest Drudgeries fit:
Made Slaves to serve their Luxury and Pride,   520
And with innumerable Hardships try'd,
Till Pitying Heav'n release us from our Pain,

Kind Heav'n to whom alone we dare complain.
Th' ill-natur'd World will no Compassion show;
Such as are wretched, it wou'd still have so: 525
It gratifies its Envy and its Spight;
The most in others Miseries take Delight.
While we are present they some Pity spare,
And Feast us on a thin Repast of Air:
Look Grave and Sigh, when we our Wrongs relate, 530
And in a Complement accuse our Fate:
Blame those to whom we our Misfortunes owe,
And all the Signs of real Friendship show.
But when we're absent, we their Sport are made,
They fan the flame, and our Oppressors aid; 535
Joyn with the Stronger, the victorious Side,
And all our Suff'rings, all our Griefs deride.
Those generous Few, whom kinder Thoughts inspire,
And who the Happiness of all desire;
Who wish we were from barbarous Usage free, 540
Exempt from Toils, and shameful Slavery,
Yet let us unreprov'd, mispend our Hours,
And to mean Purposes imploy our nobler Pow'rs.
They think if we our Thoughts can but express,
And know but how to Work, to Dance and Dress, 545
It is enough, as much as we should mind,
As if we were for nothing else design'd,
But made, like Puppets, to divert Mankind.
O that my Sex would all such Toys despise;
And only Study to be Good, and Wise: 550
Inspect themselves, and every Blemish find,
Search all the close Recesses of the Mind,
And leave no Vice, no Ruling Passion there,
Nothing to raise a Blush, or cause a Fear:
Their Memories with solid Notions fill, 555
And let their Reason dictate to their Will.
Instead of Novels, Histories peruse,
And for their Guides the wiser Ancients chuse,
Thro' all the Labyrinths of Learning go,

And grow more humble, as they more do know. 560
By doing this, they will Respect procure,
Silence the Men, and lasting Fame secure;
And to themselves the best Companions prove,
And neither fear their Malice, nor desire their Love.

Sir William. Had you the Learning you so much desire, 565
You, sure, wou'd nothing, but your selves admire:
All our Addresses wou'd be then in vain,
And we no longer in your Hearts shou'd Reign:
Sighs wou'd be lost, and Ogles cast away,
You'd laugh at all we do, and all we say. 570
No Courtship then durst by the Beaux be made
To any thing above a Chamber Maid.
Gay Cloaths, and Periwigs wou'd useless prove;
None but the Men of Sense wou'd dare to love:
With such, Heav'n knows, this Isle does not abound, 575
For one wise Man, Ten thousand Fools are found;
Who all must at an awful distance wait,
And vainly curse the rigour of their Fate.
Then blame us not if we our Interest Mind,
And would have Knowledge to our selves confin'd, 580
Since that alone Pre-eminence does give,
And rob'd of it we should unvalu'd live.
While You are ignorant, We are secure,
A little Pain will your Esteem procure.
Nonsense well cloath'd will pass for solid Sense, 585
And well pronounc'd, for matchless Eloquence:
Boldness for Learning, and a foreign Air
For nicest Breeding with th' admiring Fair.

Sir John. By Heav'n I wish 'twere by the Laws decreed
They never more should be allow'd to Read. 590
Books are the Bane of States, the Plagues of Life,
But both conjoyn'd, when studied by a Wife:
They nourish Factions, and increase Debate,
Teach needless things, and causeless Fears create.

From Plays and Novels they learn how to Plot, 595
And from your Sermons all their Cant is got:
From those they learn the damn'd intrieguing way
How to attract, and how their Snares to lay:
How to delude the Jealous Husband's Care,
Silence his Doubts, and lull asleep his Fear: 600
And when discover'd, by the Last they're taught
With Shews of Zeal to palliate their Fault;
To look Demure, and talk in such a Strain,
You'd swear they never would be ill again.

Parson. You're in the Right: Good things they misapply; 605
Yet not in Books, but them, the Fault does lie:
Plays are of use to cultivate our Parts,
They teach us how to win our Hearers Hearts:
Soft moving Language for the Pulpit's fit,
'Tis there we consecrate the Poet's Wit: 610
But Women were not for this Province made,
And shou'd not our Prerogative invade;
What e'er they know shou'd be from us convey'd:
We their Preceptors and their Guides shou'd prove,
And teach them what to hate, and what to Love. 615
But from our Sermons they no ill can learn,
They're there instructed in their true Concern;
Told what they must, and what they must not be;
And shew'd the utmost Bounds of Liberty.

Sir William. Madam, since we none of your Beauty share, 620
You shou'd content your selves with being Fair:
That is a Blessing, much more Great, than all
That we can Wisdom, or can Science call:
Such beauteous Faces, such bewitching Eyes,
Who wou'd not more than musty Authors prize? 625
Such wondrous Charms will much more Glory yield
Than all the Honours of the dusty field:
Or all those Ivy Wreaths that Wit can give,
And make you more admir'd, more reverenc'd live.

To you, the knowing World their Vows do pay, 630
And at your Feet their learned Trophies lay;
And your Commands with eager hast obey.
By all my Hopes, by all that's Good I swear,
I'd rather be some celebrated Fair,
Than wise as *Solon,* or than *Croesus* Heir. 635
Or have my Memory well stuff'd with all
Those Whimseys, which they high-rais'd notions call.

Melissa. Beauty's a Trifle merits not my Care.
I'd rather *Æsop's* ugly Visage wear,
Joyn'd with his Mind, than be a Fool, and Fair. 640
Brightness of Thought, and an extensive View
Of all the Wonders Nature has to shew;
So clear, so strong, and so inlarg'd a Sight
As can pierce thro' the gloomy Shades of Night,
Trace the first Heroes to their dark Abodes, 645
And find the Origine of Men and Gods:
See Empires rise, and Monarchies decay,
And all the Changes of the World survey:
The ancient and the modern Fate of Kings,
From whence their Glory, or Misfortune springs; 650
Wou'd please me more, than if in one combind,
I'd all the Graces of the Female Kind.
But do not think 'tis an ambitious Heat,
To you I'll leave the being Rich and Great:
Your's be the Fame, the Profit, and the Praise; 655
We'll neither Rob you of your Vines, nor Bays:
Nor will we to Dominion once aspire;
You shall be Chief, and still your selves admire.
The Tyrant Man may still possess the Throne;
'Tis in our Minds that we wou'd Rule alone: 660
Those unseen Empires give us leave to sway,
And to our Reason private Homage pay:
Our struggling Passions within Bounds confine,
And to our Thoughts their proper Tasks assign.
This, is the Use we wou'd of Knowledge make, 665

You quickly wou'd the good Effects partake.
Our Conversations it wou'd soon refine,
And in our Words, and in our Actions shine:
And by a pow'rful Influence on our Lives,
Make us good Friends, good Neighbours, and good Wives.   670
Of this, some great Examples have been shown,
Women remarkable for Virtue known:
Jealous of Honour, and upright of Life,
Serene in Dangers, and averse to Strife:
Patient when wrong'd, from Pride and Envy free,   675
Strangers to Falsehood and Calumny:
Of every noble Quality possest:
Well skill'd in Science, and with Wisdom blest.
In Ancient *Greece,* where Merit still was crown'd,
Some such as these in her Records were found.   680
Rome her *Lucretia,* and her *Porcia* show,
And we to her the fam'd *Cornelia* owe:
A Place with them does Great *Zenobia* claim;
With these I cou'd some modern Ladies Name,
Who help to fill the bulky Lists of Fame: 685
Women renown'd for Knowledge, and for Sense,
For sparkling Wit, and charming Eloquence.
But they're enough: at least to make you own,
If we less Wise and Rational are grown,
'Tis owing to your Management alone.   690
If like th' Ancients you wou'd generous prove,
And in our Education shew your Love;
Into our Souls wou'd noble Thoughts instill,
Our Infant-Minds with bright Ideas fill:
Teach us our Time in Learning to imploy,   695
And place in solid Knowledge all our Joy:
Perswade us trifling Authors to refuse,
And when we think, the useful'st Subjects chuse:
Inform us how a prosperous State to bear,
And how to Act when Fortune is severe: 700
We shou'd be Wiser, and more blameless live,
And less occasion for your Censures give:

At least in us less Failings you wou'd see,
And our Discourses wou'd less tiresom be:
Tho' Wit like yours we never hope to gain, 705
Yet from Impertinence we should refrain,
And learn to be less Talkative and Vain.
Unto the strictest Rules we should submit,
And what we ought to do, think always fit.
Never dispute, when Duty leads the way, 710
But its Commands without a Sigh Obey.
To Reason, not to Humour, give the Reins,
And be the same in Palaces and Chains.
But you our humble Suit will still decline;
To have us wise was never your Design: 715
You'll keep us Fools, that we may be your Jest;
They who know least, are ever treated best.
If we do well, with Care it is conceal'd;
But every Errour, every Fault's reveal'd:
While to each other you still partial prove, 720
Can see no Failures, and even Vices love.
The bloody Masters of the martial Trade,
Are prais'd for Mischiefs, and for Murders pay'd.
The noisy Lawyers, if they can but bawl,
Soon grace the Wool-sacks, and adorn the Hall. 725
The envy'd Great, those darling Sons of Fame,
Who carry a Majestic Terrour in their Name;
Who like the Demy Gods are plac'd on High,
And seem th' exalted Natives of the Sky:
Who sway'd by Pride, and by Self-love betray'd, 730
Are Slaves to their imperious Passions made,
Are with a Servile Awe by you rever'd;
Prais'd for their Follies, for their Vices fear'd.
The Courtier, who with every Wind can veer,
And midst the Mounting Waves can safely steer; 735
Who all can flatter; and with wond'rous grace,
Low cringing Bows, and a designing Face,
A smiling Look, and a dissembl'd Hate,
Can hug a Friend, and hasten on his Fate,

Has your Applause; his Policy you praise; 740
And to the Skies his prudent Conduct raise.
The Scholar, if he can a Verb decline,
And has the Skill to reckon Nine times Nine,
Or but the Nature of a Fly define;
Can Mouth some Greek, and knows where *Athens* stood, 745
Tho' he perhaps is neither Wise, nor Good,
Is fit for *Oxford;* where when he has been,
Each Colledge view'd, and each grave Doctor seen,
He mounts a Pulpit, and th' exalted Height
Makes Vapours dance before his troubl'd Sight, 750
And he no more can see, nor think aright.
Yet such as these your Consciences do Guide,
And or' e your Actions and your Words preside.
Blame you for Faults which they themselves commit,
Arraign your Judgment, and condemn your Wit: 755
Instil their Notions with the greatest Ease,
And Hood-wink'd lead you where so e'er they please.
The formal Justice, and the jolly Knight,
Who in their Money place their chief delight;
Who watch the Kitchin, and survey the field, 760
To see what each will to their Luxury yield:
Who Eat and Run, then Quarrel, Rail and Drink,
But never are at leisure once to Think:
Who weary of Domestick Cares being grown,
And yet, like Children, frighted when alone, 765
(Detesting Books) still Hunt, or Hawk, or Play,
And in laborious Trifles wast the Day,
Are lik'd by you, their Actions still approv'd,
And if they're Rich, are sure to be belov'd.
These are the Props, the Glory of the State, 770
And on their Nod depends the Nation's Fate:
These weave the Nets, where little Flies betray'd,
Are Victims to relentless Justice made,
While they themselves contemn the Snares that they
    have laid;
As Bonds too weak such mighty Men to hold 775

As scorn to be by any Laws controul'd.
Physicians with hard Words and haughty Looks,
And promis'd Health, bait their close-cover'd Hooks:
Like Birds of Prey, while they your Gold can scent,
You are their Care, their utmost help is lent;   780
But when your Guineas cease, you to the *Spaw* are sent,
Yet still you Court 'em, think you cannot die
If you've a Son of *Æsculapius* by.
The Tradesmen you Caress, altho' you know
They wealthy by their Cheats and Flatteries grow;   785
You seem to credit every Word they say,
And as they sell, with the same Conscience pay:
Nay to the Mob, those Dregs of Humane kind,
Those Animals you slight, you're wond'rous kind;
To them you Cring, and tho' they are your Sport,   790
Yet still you fawn, and still their Favour Court.
Thus on each other daily you impose,
And all for Wit, and dextrous Cunning goes.
'Tis we alone hard Measure still must find;
But spite of you, we'll to our selves be kind: 795
Your Censures slight, your little Tricks despise,
And make it our whole Business to be wise.
The mean low trivial Cares of Life disdain,
And Read and Think, and Think and Read again,
And on our Minds bestow the utmost Pain.   800
Our Souls with strictest Morals we'll adorn,
And all your little Arts of wheedling Scorn;
Be humble, mild, forgiving, just and true,
Sincere to all, respectful unto you,
While as becomes you, sacred Truths you teach,   805
And live those Sermons you to others Preach.
With want of Duty none shall us upbraid,
Where-e'er 'tis due, it shall be nicely pay'd.
Honour and Love we'll to our Husbands give,
And ever Constant and Obedient live: 810
If they are Ill, we'll try by gentle ways
To lay those Tempests which their Passions raise;

But if our soft Submissions are in vain,
We'll bear our Fate, and never once complain:
Unto our Friends the tenderest kindness show, 815
Be wholly theirs, no separate Interest know:
With them their Dangers and their Suff'rings share,
And make their Persons, and their Fame our Care.
The Poor we'll feed, to the Distress'd be kind,
And strive to Comfort each afflicted Mind. 820
Visit the Sick, and try their Pains to ease;
Not without Grief the meanest Wretch displease:
And by a Goodness as diffus'd as Light,
To the pursuit of Vertue all invite.
Thus will we live, regardless of your hate, 825
Till re-admitted to our former State;
Where, free from the Confinement of our Clay
In glorious Bodies we shall bask in Day,
And with inlightened Minds new Scenes survey.
Scenes, much more bright than any here below, 830
And we shall then the whole of Nature know;
See all her Springs, her secret Turnings view,
And be as knowing, and as wise as you.
With generous Spirits of a Make Divine,
In whose blest Minds Celestial Virtues shine, 835
Whose Reason, like their Station, is sublime,
And who see clearly thro' the Mists of Time,
Those puzling Glooms where busy Mortals stray,
And still grope on, but never find their way.
We shall, well-pleas'd, eternally converse, 840
And all the Sweets of Sacred Love possess:
Love, freed from all the gross Allays of Sense,
So pure, so strong, so constant, so intense,
That it shall all our Faculties imploy,
And leave no Room for any thing but Joy. 845

Notes on the Text and Sources

The Ladies Defence, published 1701.
Poems on Several Occasions, published 1703.
Poems on Several Occasions with *The Ladies Defence* added (at the end) without the author's permission, (second edition) 1709 (Lintott); reprinted 1713 with some modifications (*Ladies Defence* at the beginning) and two more editions appeared before 1750.
Essays upon Several Subjects, published 1710 (Lintott).
The Poems and Prose of Mary Lady Chudleigh, ed. Ezell, 1993, used the 1701 and 1703 editions. Here I have selected poems from Ezell's edition, retaining the order in which they first appeared—with some necessary omissions—but *The Ladies Defence* is placed at the end of the volume. There is not room in the present edition for the whole of this poem; however, because of its long-standing placement as the most famous of Chudleigh's *oeuvre*, it must be included even if only in excerpt form. Reading the poems in the 1703 edition convinces me that they were arranged by the poet in particular sequence and Chudleigh's words in the *Preface* to her essays (1710), "*When it was first Printed I had Reason to complain, but not so much as now*", ring out with the poet's displeasure with her publisher for including *Defence* in the 1709 version: that wish can be respected by keeping it low-key and at the end of the selection. However it is worth noting that, ironically, *The Ladies Defence,* which although written "*with no Design* [other than] *diverting some of my friends*", was the poem that altered the poet's status from provincial poet to that of highly acclaimed woman writer known for her defence of women's rights. Chudleigh's longest poem—which as yet has not received the critical attention it deserves—*Song of the Three Children Paraphras'd*, is also represented with an excerpt.

Notes to the Poems

On the Death of his Highness the Duke of Glocester
Title: William, Duke of Gloucester, 1689–1700, was the only child of Queen Anne to survive infancy. He died of encephalitis at the age of eleven, after developing complications from smallpox.
36. *Jove*: Roman form of Jupiter, Sovereign God of the sky.
51. *Philomela*: pastoral pen-name of the poet Elizabeth Singer Rowe; her story is told in Ovid's *Metamorphosis*.

64. *Juno's court*: in Roman myth Juno was the wife of Jupiter and Queen of the Gods.
77. *Lethe's Stream*: in Greek myth Lethe is the river of "oblivion", one of the rivers that flows through Hades; the shades of the dead had to drink from the river, so as to forget their past.
108. *British Genius*: Dryden (1631–1700), leading poet, playwright, translator and literary critic, his importance to Chudleigh as patron and friend is inestimable.
117. *Marcellus*: Marcus Claudius Marcellus (42–23 B.C.), an illustrious Roman who died when very young; was descended from a famous Roman General of the same name; Virgil introduces him in Book VI of the *Aeneid* when Aeneas sees him in the underworld. Plutarch wrote *The Life of Marcellus* and this was translated by Dryden in 1683.
119. *Maro*: Publius Vergilius Maro, the classical Roman poet Virgil (70–19 B.C.); Dryden translated his works in 1697.
127–132. *Ascanius*: son of Aeneas; was an important symbol of his father's destiny as founder of Rome; proves his mettle at a young age when he steps in to defend Troy in the Trojan War; after the fall of Troy he and Aeneas escape to Italy. 129: *Tyrian Queen*: Dido, Queen of Carthage; in the *Aeneid* Venus replaces Ascanius with her son Cupid, God of love, so that Dido will fall in love with Aeneas.
175–6. *Aegeus*: in Greek myth an Athenian King and father of Theseus; presuming Theseus dead Aegeus killed himself in despair after his son's ship returned from Crete, flying black, rather than the white sails he'd promised his father if he succeeded in his plan to slay the Minotaur.
195–202. *Andromache . . . Son:* in Greek myth was the wife of Hector, the Trojan warrior; *Astyanax* was one of their sons; after the fall of Troy Andromache, who was the epitome of a virtuous Greek wife, initially saved her young son from death, only to find that he had been thrown from the city walls by Ulysses.
203. *Brittania:* personification of Britain.
205. *Sylvan Throng:* deities or spirits of the woods.
227. *Nereids*: sea-nymphs or Goddesses, patrons of sailors and fishermen who came to the aid of men in trouble.
239. *Thracian Bard*: in myth, Orpheus, who turned and looked back at Eurydice as they left Hades and therefore lost her for ever.
259. *Guardian of our Isle*: St George.
269-78. The young Duke's entry into heaven (*Æthereal Shore*) emphasises his regal inheritance as being as significant as that of the Stuart King

(*Caledonian Chiefs*) martyrs and further, places him in their Royal lineage.
279. *Danish Heroes*: Vikings; a line in *Beowulf* reads: "We've heard of Danish Heroes/Ancient kings and the glory they cut/for themselves, swinging mighty swords!"
286. *beauteous suff'ring Queen*: Mary Queen of Scots (1542–87), executed by order of her cousin Elizabeth I.
291. *dearest Off-spring took*: James VI of Scotland / I of England (1566–1625).
292. *martyr'd Prince*: Charles I, King of England (1625–49), who was executed by Parliament.
302. *his Son*: Charles II, King of England, 1660–85.
304. *Maria*: Queen Mary, wife of William and child of James II, she reigned 1689–94.

On the Vanities of this Life: A Pindarick Ode
Title: first of several poems by Chudleigh using this form which, named after Pindar, was generally characterised by its ceremonious formal structure of triadic strophe, anti-strophe and epode; Pindaric odes were popularised by Abraham Cowley and Dryden. See also *A Pindaric Ode*, *The Observation* and *Song of the Three Children*. Chudleigh noted in her *Preface* to the latter poem that she found the Pindaric form allowed her the "liberty of running into large Digressions" and that it "gives a great Scope to the Fancy".
36. *Harpies*: in Greek myth, they were beautiful, winged maidens, but were later described as winged monsters with the faces of ugly old women and baring sharp talons. They were supposed to carry people off to the underworld to torture them.
92. *Antepasts*: foretastes.
109. *Seraphick*: relating to angels.
195. *Phoenix Truth*: the Phoenix has been used as a Christian symbol of regeneration; in legend it is the bird reborn from its own ashes.

To Almystrea
Title. *Almystrea:* The first poem in the selection written to a woman within Chudleigh's literary circle using a pastoral pen-name; this is an anagram of Mary Astell, writer of *A Serious Proposal to the Ladies* (1694) and *Some Reflections Upon Marriage* (1700). The placement of this poem near the opening of the collection, and its deferential tone, indicate the importance of Astell's work for Chudleigh.
1. *Marissa*: Chudleigh's own *nom de plume*.

To Clorissa:
Title. The second poem addressed to a female friend by means of a pseudo-pastoral name contrasts with the previous one. *Clorissa*'s actual identity has not yet been revealed, but the poem suggests she was a close friend of Chudleigh's.
34–6. Compare with lines 23–5 of *On the Death;* Chudleigh emphasises the importance of reading for women.
46–7. The poem turns on the notion of the interrelatedness between the sacredness of the friendship and its erotic overtones.
66–67/72–3. The association of "thoughts" and "interests" with lines 24-5 implies that the mutual intensity of feeling and thought between the two women will aid in their composition of poetry, which will thus be enhanced by their dual effort.

To Mr Dryden on his excellent Translation of Virgil
Title. Dryden's translated edition of the works of Virgil was published in 1697. There is a tradition that Dryden completed his translation whilst staying at Ugbrooke Park with the Cliffords.
1–5. Compare the tone with *To Almystrea*; in both poems the poet has deliberately presented her own gifts as less worthy than those of her dedicatees: in this homage she professes her humility. She is deliberately keeping her role as writer very low key, though as with other women writing at the same time, would probably have had high professional ambitions for her own work. This duplicitous stance protects her, because of its apparent deference to the status quo, within a culture where female poets are still establishing their position.
23–43. A chronological panoply of a selection of male canonical writers from Chaucer to Cowley, with Dryden recognised as representing the pinnacle of literary achievement. *Spencer*: Edmund Spenser (ca. 1552–99), known for his pastoral lyric poetry, in particular, the *Shepheard's Calendar* and *The Fairie Queen*; *Waller*: Edmund Waller, M.P. and lyric poet (1606–87), *Poems of Waller*, 1645; *Divine Poems*, 1685; was regarded as the pioneer who introduced the heroic couplet into English verse; *Milton*: John Milton (1608–74), major poet, his *Lycidas* was written in the pastoral convention; *Cowley*: Abraham Cowley, poet and founder of the Royal Society (1618–67): was the most famous poet of the time; known for his metaphysical poetry and for creating the Pindaric ode used by Dryden and other successors; in his lifetime his fame superseded that of his contemporary Milton's parallel career.

45–6. This may refer to Ugbrooke, because of its associations with Dryden and his work on Virgil, and in particular to "Dryden's seat", a grassy knoll near Ugbrooke, where he is supposed to have written *The Hind and the Panther,* published in 1687. From this hill there were dramatic views of the Devonshire countryside.
47. *Acquests.* Acquistions.
62. Equivalent to the Christian Heaven, the *"Elysian fields"* in Greek mythology were the final resting places for the souls of the heroic and virtuous.
68–70. Augeas, King of Greece, had the largest stable in the country; it had never been cleaned until Hercules was given that task, as the fifth of his twelve labours.
72. From the beginning of the C17 *Gothic/k,* which originally referred to the language of the Goths, began to take on a wider interpretation: here it signifies "barbaric" rather than "medieval," its principal meaning.

Song

A few short lyrics thread the original collection—perhaps they were interspersed for light relief. This serves as a foil, sandwiched between the previous panegyric to Dryden (a male mentor) and the poem which follows it (a female "muse"). Its mockery of the conventions of courtly love sublimates the poet's more serious message.

To Eugenia

Title. Eugenia's identity is uncertain. As named writer of *The Female Advocate* (1700), she was until recently thought to be Chudleigh herself, but here she is named as another dedicatee of the poet's. Another so far unidentified female contemporary poet, *Ephelia,* also wrote a poem to Eugenia: *To the Honoured Eugenia, commanding me to write to her,* but it is not known if this is the same Eugenia as Chudleigh is addressing.

1. *Golden Age.* The poem highlights the contrast between the period of superficial "gold and beauty" ridiculed in the previous poem and the "Golden Age", the idyllic paradise defined within pastoral modes, where "virtue" was supposedly a pre-eminent quality. The poem implies that Eugenia's work was exemplary in its depiction of that idyll.

The Wish
One of the few poems whose subject is male, this poem revises Abraham Cowley's poem of the same name; its placement—after the previous clutch of poems, which celebrate and explicate female companionship in its various guises—is telling: the absence, lack of and longing for a reciprocal male friend who embodies the moral qualities here defined, is made more poignant.

The Elevation
Contains a Donne-like metaphysical conceit: compare with *A Valediction: Forbidding Mourning* or *The Extasie*. Framed in between the two friendship-wish poems this poem emphasises the poet's self-sufficient ambitions: her soul is envisioned as female, free-wheeling and ennobled. The poem is informed by neoplatonic theories, influenced by the C17 Cambridge Platonist revival—the soul, in ecstasy, is empowered to transcend all worldly constructs.
1–2. Compare with lines 3–6 of *To Alymstrea*.

Friendship
5. *Whose souls combine*: Chudleigh's version of neoplatonism unsettles Donne's ideal of the two-souls-as-one depicted in such poems as *Valediction*: both *The Wish* and *Friendship* describe the absence of that ideal and instead imply that fulfilment can only be attained for the unique and individual soul/spirit.

The Happy Man
The poem revises translations/poems of both Dryden (*Happy the Man*) and Cowley (*Solitude*), which themselves were written in the tradition of the C7 Latin lyric poet Horace's concept of the *beatus vir*: it appears in his Ode 29, book 3 (the "Happy Man", who away from the corruptions of town and city could retire into a private rural retreat and there contemplate and cherish his own soul).
13. *Halycon*: peaceful and still idyll (the seven days in Winter when storms were not supposed to occur), named from the Greek myth of Alycone and Ceyx.

To the Ladies
The most anthologized of Chudleigh's poems, a shorter, concise companion to *The Ladies Defence* and the most succinct statement of her proto-feminist beliefs, with its negative views on matrimony. Aimed both at women who have already succumbed to marriage and as a warning to

those not yet wed, the poem works by way of its metaphoric linking of "wife" and "servant" and its condescending tone. Chudleigh's advice is stark: she is not deluded into believing that men will be persuaded to alter their behaviour, so it is for the woman to avoid the "wretched State" (21). Telling perhaps is its position at the end of the first group of poems and just before the second of the poems addressed *To the Queen*. The derisory vision this poem has of the dynamic between husband and wife contrasts with Chudleigh's idealistic partnership, as depicted in *The Wish*.

To the Queen's most Excellent Majesty
Title: Second and middle of Chudleigh's panegyrics to Queen Anne, the poet frames the poem in the guise of praise for the new Queen, whilst steering her towards adopting her predecessor's policies.
31. *Gallick Foe*: predicts Anne's resistance to French control and renewed Catholicism.
34. *Tread in his Steps*: William III died in 1702.
60. *Salic Laws . . . Gallick throne*: French law prohibited women from taking the throne.
124. Albion: England.

The Resolution
Strategically placed at the centre of the original *Poems on Several Occasions*, the poem is also the longest of that collection and seems thus implicitly significant. An array of classical and literary references is undercut by a hidden agenda, which promotes female resolution and self-sacrifice.
1. *Philistris*: identity unknown.
21. *Rochester/Athens's Plague*: probably Thomas Sprat (1636–1713), son of a clergyman, born at Tallaton in Devon; became Bishop of Rochester, 1684; author of *The Plague of Athens*.
27. *Stillingfleet*: Edward Stillingfleet, Bishop of Worcester (1635–99); highly respected Churchman; engaged in scholarly debate in correspondence with Locke; almost assassinated during the Popish Plot 1678, whilst Dean of St Paul's.
29. *Tillotson*: Archbishop of Canterbury (1630–94); his sermons were extremely popular throughout the country; both he and Stillingfleet were principle latitudinarians.
35. *Sarum*: Gilbert Burnet, Bishop of Salisbury (1643–1715); Scottish theologian, historian and writer; volume one of his *History of the Reformation of the Church of England* was published in 1679.
48. *Norris*: John Norris, Platonist (1657–1711); Rector at Newton-St Loe in Somerset for two years, where he published *Christian*

Blessedness, one of his most popular works, in 1690; Rector of Bemerton 1691; many other publications; was influenced by the Cambridge Platonists; corresponded with various people within Chudleigh's literary circle, including Mary Astell, Elizabeth Thomas and Chudleigh herself; he critiqued Locke's work of 1690, *An Essay Concerning Human Understanding*, by way of the philosophy of the French Platonist Malebranche.

79. *Socrates*: 469–399; Greek Philosopher who set the standard for all philosophers who followed him; Plato's mentor, he became a controversial political figure. Following a trial at which he received a death sentence, he took hemlock and died, stoically accepting his fate.

126. *Saturn's Golden Reign*: there are numerous references in classical texts expressing nostalgia for the so called utopian Golden Age: in 1693 Dryden had translated Ovid's *Metamorphoses*, in which Saturn's reign, the first of the four ages of time, is presented as the pastoral idyll which has since characterised its presentation in literature; phrase appears in Cowley's poem *Plantarum*, 1683.

138. *Regulus*: Marcus Regulus, Roman consul (3rd century B.C.), who put public interest before his own life when he chose to return to Carthage to certain torture and death, rather than break his word.

139. *Aristrides*: Athenian soldier and statesmen (530–468 B.C.), who was known for his scrupulous honesty and nicknamed "The Just"; loved by the Athenians, but never received the proper honours for his public service; at one time was ostracised and banished from the city, but this penalty was later revoked.

141. *Cato*: a Stoic (5th Century B.C.), known for his integrity, stubbornness and contempt for the corruption of his period; committed suicide rather than accept the authority of Julius Caesar, against whom he had for many years maintained a campaign of moral antagonism.

147–73. *Petus* and *Arria*: Paetus, a Roman senator (5th Century B.C.), was condemned to death for being involved in a conspiracy against Claudius; his wife, Arria, stabbed herself and passed the sword to her husband who, inspired by her example, followed suit. Chudleigh expands Arria's story and presents her telling Paetus stories about other exemplary and brave Romans, *Curtius*, the *Decii* and *Brutus*, before taking the ultimate action of suicide by sword.

174. *Epictetus*: a Stoic (A.D. 60–140), born a slave but eventually gained his freedom; his philosophy guided the individual towards the achievement of a state of self-regulated inner calm and tranquillity; his works were collected by his student Arrianus as *Discourses* and

the shorter, epigrammatic, *Enchiridion*. *Nero*: Roman Emperor (A.D.54–68), freed Epictetus, but was himself noted for barbaric cruelty, though some have suggested that he was popular with the Romans.

176. *Belisarius*: one of the greatest military commanders of the Byzantine Empire (A.D. 527–63), his success in reconquering the Roman Empire brought him many enemies: accused of conspiracy, after having his eyes put out he was reduced to begging in the streets.

191–2. *Assyrian—Babel's lofty Tow'rs*: by the 9th century B.C. the Assyrians had grown to control most of the Middle East; they were finally overcome by the Babylonians in 609B.C.

193. *Cyrus*: Cyrus, as King of Persia, took the city of Babylon, 539 B.C.

195. *Darius*: one of Cyrus' successors; in 331 B.C. Darius III was defeated by Alexander the Great and lost Babylon.

196. *Pellean Youth*: Alexander the Great (356–323 B.C.).

199. *Ammon*: in 332B.C. Alexander the Great consulted Ammon, the Oracle God at his sanctuary and was supposedly informed that he himself was a God, son of Ammon.

208. *Expansum*: from Latin: a wide space, or wide arch of sky.

209. *Royal Shepherds*: the twin infants Romulus and Remus restored Numitor, their Grandfather, as King of the city that was to become Rome; a miraculous intervention of a shepherd aided them in their success; eventually Romulus slew his brother after a dispute re the naming and ruling of Rome.

225. *Lucretia*: quintessentially virtuous wife of Tarquinius: a legendary female; her rape by Tarquin and resultant suicide were the causes of the overthrow of the monarchy and establishment of the Roman Republic.

248. *Caesar*: Julius Caesar, assassinated in 44 B.C., had ruled Rome for four years.

267. *Pompey*: Pompey, Roman General (106–48 B.C.), who with Caesar and Crassus initiated the first triumvirate; later he and Caesar became rivals and Pompey was assassinated by Septimus.

268. *Aniellos*: son of a C17 fisherman who led a popular revolt in Naples and was afterwards elected Captain of the people.

275. *Homer/Grecians*: Homer, Greek poet (9th Century B.C.), who is attributed with the authorship of *The Iliad,* which relates the story of the siege of Troy.

276. Agamemnon, King of Mycenae, is *the King*, brother of Menelaus, the *injur'd Husband* of Helen: The Trojan War began after Paris stole Helen and took her to Troy.

277. *Ilium*: Troy.

278–80. *for her sake . . . Country stood:* Hecuba was the mother of many of the men who were killed during the War, including Hector.

282. *Phrygians:* Trojans.

284–89: *Achilles-Trojan Walls:* in *The Iliad* Achilles withdrew from the Trojan War after Agamemnon took Chryseis, his slave girl, but returned to battle after his best friend was killed by the great Trojan hero Hector; Achilles kills Hector and drags his body around the walls of Troy.

290. *Cyprian Goddess:* Aphrodite, Greek Goddess, who in *The Iliad* aids the Trojans and also protects Hector.

291. *Idalian Plain:* Cyprus.

292–301. *Ulysses—Love:* these lines refer to Homer's other epic, *The Odyssey,* in which the homecoming of another Greek hero, Odysseus, is related.

295–301: Odysseus' wife Penelope was *his lov'd Princess* who waited over twenty years for him to return, keeping her other suitors at bay.

302–17: *Prince of Lyrick—ev'ry Ode:* Pindar (522–443 B.C.), regarded by some as the greatest of the Greek lyric poets; spent much of his life writing victory odes in honor of the winners of various games, including the *45 Victory Odes;* also composed paeans and other hymns for religious festivals.

320. *Twice save his House . . . Thebes:* Alexander the Great left Pindar's house untouched when he destroyed Thebes in 335 B.C.

323–37. *Tyrtaeus:* was a Greek elegiac poet (7th century B.C.), who lived in *Sparta;* his martial elegiac poems were supposed to have been written to urge Spartan soldiers to victory. *Mars* was the Roman God of War and *Messene* a city conquered by the Spartans.

338-39: *Theocritus-Sicilian Swains:* Greek poet (ca. 350–250 B.C.), thought to be founder of the pastoral genre of poetry; his *Idylls* describe Sicilian life.

348. *Lucretius:* Lucretius Carus, Epicurean poet, (d. ca. 50 B.C.), wrote a six-book poem *De Rerum Natura* (On the Nature of Things), which, expounding Epicurean beliefs, uses rational argument to present a view of the world governed by natural phenomena (the interactions of groups of tiny atoms), rather than the will of the Gods; he proposes that peace and contentment are derived from the pursuit of virtue. Dryden translated the work in 1685.

381. *Virgil:* classical Roman poet (70–19B.C.); in 1697 Dryden had translated his *Pastorals, Georgics* and *The Aeneid.*

386. *Silenus's Song:* in Virgil's *Eclogue* 6, Silenus sings the story of the creation of the world; Silenus had poetic gifts, as he was supposed to possess wisdom and the power of prophecy.

395–7. *Alcides*: in Greek myth, Heracles; in Roman myth known as Hercules, son of Zeus and Alcemena; *Juno*, hostile to the mortal children of her husband Zeus (Jupiter), was vindictive to him from his birth.

400–3. *Horace* . . . *Heat inspire*: (Quintus Horatius Flaccus), a Roman lyric poet (65–8 B.C.); his *Odes* and verse *Epistles* promote the pleasures of the simple life and retirement from public life; his *Ars Poetica*, which discussed the art of poetry, had a significant influence on later poets. Chudleigh adopts the then current stance of appreciation of the classical poets for their gift of wild inspiration: the fire of their poetic muse was far superior to the "empty song" of many C17/18 poets.

409. *Ovid*: ranked with Virgil and Horace as one of the trio of most important canonical poets of classical literature, Publius Ovidius Naso (Ovid, 43 B.C.–17A.D.) was remembered for the epic poem *Metamorphoses*, which was based on Greek myth.

422. *Golden Apple*: Venus, the goddess of love, gave Hippomenes, one of the huntress Atalanta's suitors, the three golden apples to strew in her path, so that she would pick them up and consequently lose a race against him; he could then win her in marriage.

423. *Eurydice*: the wife of Orpheus, who broke his vow and turned back to look at her in Hades, whereupon she vanished forever.

424. *pond'rous Torment roll*: the King *Sisyphus* who, in Greek myth, was punished by having to roll a large rock up a hill throughout eternity.

427. *Pluto*: Roman mythological god of the underworld.

429. *calcin'd*: short for calcination: in alchemy one of the twelve vital processes necessary for transformation of a substance.

436–7. Refers to Dryden's translation of Ovid's *Heroides*, 1680. In the *Heroides* Ovid had composed a series of fictitious letters, supposedly sent by abandoned or desperate heroines to the men who had rejected them: they are in the form of tragic monologues.

438. *Oenone*: *Oenone to Paris*, (*Heroides V*); in Greek myth Oenone, a mountain nymph and lover of Paris, is abandoned and betrayed by him for Helen: later, she commits suicide, haunted with remorse after refusing to aid him when he is mortally wounded; in the *Heroides* she reproaches Paris for his desertion.

440. *Hypermnestra:* in myth Hypermnestra is constantly torn between her father Danaus and Lynceus, her lover: she refuses to fulfil her father's order to kill Lynceus and rescues him instead, because of her innate sense of responsibility; in *Heroides XIV*, Hypermnestra has been

thrown into prison by her father for her betrayal; bound by chains she writes to Lynceus, asking for his help.

441. *Phyllis*: in myth Phyllis fell into despair after her lover Demophoon failed to return to her, and hanged herself, only to be changed into an almond tree; in *Heroides II*, Phyllis writes a letter to Demophoon just before her suicide.

442. *Laodamia*: in myth is married to Protesilaus, who has sailed off as a warrior in the Trojan War; after she learns of his death, she kills herself; in *Heroides XIII*, full of foreboding, she writes to him just before he dies.

443. *Sappho/Phaon*: the Greek poet who, after being rejected by Phaon, is said to have flung herself over a cliff; Ovid gave Sappho a monologue in *Heroides XV;* in it she says that she "burns like Etna".

454–455: *Juvenal . . . Persius*: the last of the great Roman satirists, (A.D. 1–2); Dryden translated their satires in 1692.

460. *Phoebus*: in classical myth is Apollo, god of the sun and poetry.

462–464: *Milton . . . Roscommon*: Milton (1608–74): Phoebus appears in *Lycidas*: "Phoebus touch'd my trembling ears", reminding him that earthly fame is illusory and that only in heaven is there lasting renown; *Denham*: Sir John Denham, poet, translator and satirist (1615–69), known for his poem *Cooper's Hill* (1642), which is the first example of a long topographical poem; *Waller*: Edmund Waller, M.P. and lyric poet (1606–87), *Poems of Waller*, 1645 and *Divine Poems*, 1685—regarded by some as the pioneer who introduced the heroic couplet into English verse; *Roscommon*: Wentworth Dillon, 4th Earl of Roscommon (ca. 1630–85), English poet who translated Horace's *Ars Poetica* into blank verse (1680)—renowned for his *Essay on Translated Verse* (1684), which was the first account of the principles of poetic diction.

465–470. *Dryden . . . he is gone*: Dryden died in 1700.

473. *Dorset*: Charles Sackville, 6th Earl of Dorset (1638-1706), poet, satirist and courtier; friend and patron to Earl of Halifax; Privy Counsellor and Lord Chamberlain to William of Orange; his poems were praised by Dryden.

474. *Normanby*: John Sheffield, 3rd Earl of Mulgrave, and 1st Duke of Buckingham and Normanby (1648–1721), English statesman and author of numerous poems, *An Essay on Satire* (1680) and *An Essay upon Poetry* (1682).

475. *Halifax*: Charles Montagu, Earl of Halifax (1661–1715), English poet and statesman: wrote *An Epistle to Charles Earl of Dorset occasioned by King William's Victory in Ireland*, 1690.

480. *Granville*: George Granville, Lord Lansdowne (1667–1735), poet, playwright and politician; his play *Heroic Love; or The Cruel Separation* (1698), shows Dryden's influence and is drawn from the story of Agamemnon and Chryseis in the Homeric tales of heroic love.

489-492. *Chryseis ... Atrides*: In *The Iliad*, during the battle of Troy, Chryseis is taken by Agamemnon (Atrides) as concubine. In Granville's play, *Chryseis* is described as 'the brightest Pattern of Heroic Love/and perfect Virtue, that the World e'er knew'. Chudleigh's emphasis is on the qualities of the female character within the play and her archetypal representation of goodness.

513–4. *Dennis*: John Dennis (1657–1734), a dramatist, literary critic and another acquaintance of Dryden's. Chudleigh is probably referring to his critical work, *The Advancement and Reformation of Modern Poetry* (1701), in which, using a specifically Christian framework, he synthesises classical, aesthetic and philosophical elements in order to combine poetry and religion that would in turn effect political change.

515–18. *Vanbrook*: Sir John Vanbrugh (1624–1726), architect and radical dramatist who wrote several popular Restoration comedies. Known for their sexual explicitness and defence of women's rights, his plays offended some sections of society; because of criticism he turned from writing to garden design and architecture. *The Relapse* was performed in 1696 and *Aesop*—in which Aesop is figured as a fashionable Restoration courtier—in 1696–7. In mythology *Thersites* was a rank-and-file soldier of the Greek army during the Trojan War; he mocked Achilles for falling in love with Penthesilea, whereupon Achilles flew into a rage and killed him. There were similarities between Thersites and Aesop, as both were satirists and both died as a consequence of their abusive behaviour.

519–30. *Garth*: leading Physician of the Whigs and poet (1661–1719), Samuel Garth was a satirist and translator; he produced a eulogy at Dryden's funeral. His satire and mock-epic *The Dispensary* (1699), which creates a mock Homeric contest between physicians and apothecaries, was very popular in his day and before this, in 1697, he had given his *Harveian Oration*; he also wrote *Claremont*, a moralising poem. Pope called Garth the "best good Christian, without knowing it". In *The Dispensary* Garth appropriates epic names and themes from *The Aeneid* in a passage which celebrates Rome's heroes: *Camillus*, *Fabius* and *Scipio* appear.

531. *Nassau*: King William III, praised in *The Dispensary*.

533. *Phlegraean Plain*: from Ovid's *Metamorphoses*; in classical myth, the site of a battle.

535. *Minerva*: Queen Anne, who had taken the throne in March 1702, after William III's death: Minerva or Pallas Athene was the Roman name of the Greek goddess of wisdom, war and art.
537. *Congreve*: William Congreve (1670–1729), was an English dramatist, taught by Dryden, who wrote both tragedies and comedies, but became known for the latter—particularly *Love for Love* (1695) and *The Way of the World* (1700).
538. *Almeria*: the heroine from Congreve's tragedy *The Mourning Bride* opens the play with the lines "Music has charms to sooth a savage breast".
539–45. *Homer—Hecuba*: in 1693 Dryden published *Examen Poeticum*, translations of part of Homer's *Iliad*, some of which had been written by Congreve, his then protégé. The sections by Congreve included *Priam's Lamentation* and *Petition to Achilles, For the Body of his Son Hector* and *The Lamentations of Hecuba, Andromache and Helen* and *Over the Dead Body of Hector*. Chudleigh's identification is with the female characters Andromache and Hecuba. She may have been influenced by Dryden's suggestion, in his introduction to the translations, that Congreve's rendering of the tragedies gave more poignancy and depth than the original Homer: "If this last [Priam's lamentation over the death of Hector] excite compassion in you, as I doubt not but it will, you are more obliged to the translator than the poet".
550–574. *Rowe:* this section draws material from the play *Tamerlane* (1702), the second drama written by the poet and dramatist Nicholas Rowe (1674–1718); the play was immensely popular in its day and made Rowe's reputation as writer of tragedies; it is based on the Mongol (*Scythian*) conqueror of Western Asia, Amir Temur, who represents William III, whilst *Bajazet* satirizes Louis XIV; for many years *Tamerlane* was re-enacted on the anniversary of William and Mary's landing at Brixham, 1688, so may have had special local significance for Chudleigh. Rowe's plays presented strong female characters, indicating his interest in a degree of female independence: the women drive the narrative, although the main plot turns on the relationship between Tamerlane and Bajazet: hence this is an equivalent device to that used by Chudleigh in this poem, where the sub-text promotes female integrity and resolution.
564. *Arpasia*: taken by Bajazet to be his lover, even though she is married to Moneses; Bajazet has Moneses strangled in front of her; she is shown to be stoically resolute in facing her fate.
571–4 *Selima*: beautiful daughter of Bajazet, rescued by *Axalla,* a Christian, who is Tamerlane's general.

584–90. *Montezuma-Amazon*: Montezuma, principal hero of Robert Howard's and Dryden's play, *The Indian Queen* (1664) and its sequel, *The Indian Emperor* (1667); Montezuma, revealed in the plays as the long-lost Mexican Emperor, marries the Inca's daughter. As Dryden's writings have already appeared in this poem, Chudleigh could have been referring to *Accosta*, a classic work of New World history, which was originally published in 1590: this contained the observations of Accosta, a Spanish Jesuit missionary in Peru and Mexico, so may have related the exploits of Montezuma.

591. *Asiatick Pride*: appears in *Canidia*, an eccentric satire, published in 1683, and attributed to the royalist divine, Robert Dixon.

606. *Confutius*: Confucius, the Chinese Philosopher and thinker, 551–479 B.C.

630. *Narcissus*: infamous in mythology. He rejected all the nymphs and girls who fell in love with him, including Echo, and instead became preoccupied with his own reflection, doomed eventually to perish there. The narcissus flower sprang up at the site.

A Pindarick Ode

1–5. *Syrens*: half women, half birds, the Sirens appear in the *Odyssey*.

6. *"sweet enticing Lays"*: the Sirens' songs (Lays) enticed seamen to their death. Compare with last line of the poem, "designing, meaner Lays".

10. Odysseus escaped the Sirens' clutches by having himself tied to the ship's mast, so that he could not jump overboard and follow their song.

26. *Their Plumes the Muses now adorn*: the Sirens challenged the Muses with a song contest, which they lost, whereupon the Muses removed their wings/plumes. The Muses banished the Sirens, who, humiliated, left the mainland for islands in the middle of the sea.

29. *Ulysses*: Odysseus.

33–4. *Orpheus*: legendary Greek poet whose playing of the lyre was said to charm whoever or whatever heard it. His music even helped the Argonauts resist the Sirens' enticements.

63. *harmonious Numbers*: Dryden, commenting on the diction within his translation of Virgil, claims that his version has the "harmony of numbers", which were lacking in previous translations. Chudleigh may be suggesting that the writer who has attained the state of inner poise will be best placed to follow Dryden's example and able to write comparably felicitous verse.

To the Learn'd and Ingenious Dr. Musgrave of Exeter
Title: *Dr William Musgrave*, (1665–1721), settled in Exeter in 1691; remembered for his works about arthritis and as a leading antiquarian; is reputed to have had an extensive library; he practised in an alley off the North side of the High Street, which was later named after him.
17. *Lov'd Daughter*: Chudleigh's youngest child, Eliza Maria (see *On the Death of My Dear Daughter*).
77. *Aesculapius*: in Greek and Roman mythology, god of healing and medicine.

The Observation
Both this and the following poem are Pindaric and both are influenced by Chudleigh's engagement with neoplatonic thought.

Solitude
6. *Confining Clay:* see the "heavy lump" (line 59), of *Observation*, which ends that poem with an essentially nihilistic view of human beings. Here that same image is used to present the ideal of the soul in retreat-mode, enabled via self-determination to rise away from, and above the discarded body, into transcendent bliss.
12. *Seraphick:* angelic.
27. *Embryo of the World*: chaos or world-seed.
62. *Sportive Goddess*: probably Athena.
99. Reason is feminised; see also *The Resolve*.

On the Death of my Honoured Mother Mrs Lee: A Dialogue between Lucinda and Marissa
Title: *Lucinda's* identity is unknown. Chudleigh's mother was Mary Lee, née Sydenham, from Wynford Eagle in Dorset. Many of the Sydenhams were eminent figures in the fields of medicine, science and philosophy.
73. *Stoicks*: Stoics were members of a philosophical school whose theory revolved round the self-discipline achieved by means of concentration, reason and reflection.
90. *Philanda:'s name*: Mary Lee.
128. *Antepast*: foretaste.

On the Death of my dear Daughter Eliza Maria Chudleigh
Title: Eliza was Chudleigh's youngest child: she was born in 1693 and died in 1701/2 after a long battle with illness (see *To the Learn'd and*

Ingenious Dr. Musgrave of Exeter). Chudleigh's eldest child, also Mary, had lived less than a year (September, 1676–January, 1677); her son Richard died at the age of three (1688): only two of her six children survived into adulthood.

The Offering
Title: in the form of a direct dedication to God, the poem suggests a change of direction for the poet, a renewal of affirmation after philosophical debate and dialogue. It seems to pre-figure *Song of the Three Children Paraphras'd* in its blend of rational science and theology.

14–40. *restless Atoms play*: an image used frequently by the poet; it refers to the "atomic" theory of the Roman poet and naturalist Lucretius, who, deriving ideas from Epicurus, stated that only two realities exist, solid, everlasting particles and the void. Lucretius's theories were outlined in the poem *De Rarum Natura*, (*On the Nature of Things*), which Dryden translated. See also *Resolution*, note 348.

The Resolve
Title: in the tradition of the "beatus vir" in which retreat provides an opportunity for self-improvement (see *The Happy Man*).

5–8. Feminised "reason" is figured as a "queen"; Chudleigh's gendering contradicts the then conventional assumption of maleness and rationality.

One of Lucian's Dialogues of the Dead Paraphras'd
Title: Lucian was a Greek satirist (A.D 125–180), best remembered for his *The Dialogues of the Dead*, a model of Greek wit and polish; in form these used the Platonic conversational mode. This is a paraphrase of *Dialogue 1,* between *Diogenes* (a character in the *Dialogues* based on the celebrated Cynic philosopher) and *Pollux* (based on the son of Jupiter and brother of Castor). Diogenes orders Pollux to invite *Menippus* (Cynic philosopher and chief satirical spokesman of the *Dialogues*) down to Hades as there he will have more chance for mirth—here *Diogones* says that you can laugh heartily without a second thought.

29. *Bacchus*: God of wine.
79. *Megilbus*: probably *Megillus*, cross-gendered, who appears in Lucian's *Dialogues of the Courtesan*.
80. *Damoxenus*: a boxer of Syracuse, who was excluded from fights after he had killed an opponent.

97. *Stygian*: dark and dismal, relating to the river Styx in Hades.
106. *Sparta*: city state in ancient Greece.
117. *Hermes*: a shifty figure, messenger God or God of boundaries and of those who travel through them.
118. *Orphean Lyre*: the lyre was invented by Hermes, but was eventually acquired by Orpheus; its music could charm both beast and man.

To the Queen's most Excellent Majesty

10-13 *Trojan*: Aeneas, hero of Virgil's *Aeneid* and mortal Prince, who escaped to *Latium* in Italy after the Trojan Wars. According to Virgil, he was involved in the founding of Rome. Chudleigh presents him as role-model for the Queen.
41-74. *Virgin Glory*: Elizabeth I; the most extended allusion in this poem, which points out parallels between the two Queens: each had to establish her own merit as worthy Sovereign, as well as maintain her reign, given that neither of them had an heir.
45. *Sister's hate*: Mary Tudor.
91. *Gallick Arms*: French influence and power.
95. *Iberian Shore—destin'd prey*: south-west Europe, which includes modern day Portugal, Spain, Gibraltar, Andorra and a small part of France. From 95–112, Chudleigh is advocating the continued role of the English on the continent against the French, after the establishment of the Grand Alliance, the European coalition that had been set up under William. *The Belgick Lion*: the heraldic emblem of the Netherlands, therefore associated with William and his family, embodied the motto, "He menaces the Sun but protects the earth".
116. *Pallas*: Athena, Goddess of Wisdom.
121. *Phoebus*: Apollo, God of Wisdom. Perhaps Chudleigh is suggesting that Anne's exemplary reign will embody the best of both male and female qualities or virtues.

Song of the Three Children

The longest poem in *Poems on Several Occasions* presents multiple themes, but is based on an apocryphal addition to the Book of Daniel, where the three young men are cast into the fiery furnace by King Nebuchadnezzar: one of them praises the Lord for saving them. The poem, in the form of a Pindaric ode, extends themes and ideas appearing in *The Resolution*. It focuses on many of Chudleigh's most noticeable concerns—particularly her engagement with what Ezell calls "rational theology", in which the poet presents scintillating and sensual descriptions; these interpret the "song of science" from a Christian viewpoint. The poem deserves far more attention than can be given here; the excerpt is just a taster.

Nos. 22–24
531. *Sabæan sweets*: the city of Saba, in Arabia Felix, was renowned for its perfumed spices, especially incense.
542. *Hesperian Gardens*: in Ovid's *Metamorphosis*, the faraway paradise, or legendary orchard, at the edge of the world, where the golden apples grew.
544. *Mæonides*. Homer was sometimes called the Mæonian bard.
545-9. *Alcinous garden*: Alcinous was King of the island of Phæacia, and in *The Odyssey* entertained Odysseus after he was washed onto the island's shores; Phæacia was famed for its paradisal palace gardens.
557. Virgil's *Eclogues* describe a tranquil pastoral haven.

The Ladies Defence

This long poem—which Chudleigh called a "Satyr on Vice"—was written in response to a sermon by John Sprint, itself published as *The Bride-Woman's Counsellor* two years previously; it was not the only text penned by a woman reacting to that sermon's vehement misogyny. It is likely that Chudleigh was aware of the other author/s and may even have been well acquainted with her/them. Indeed, until recently these other pamphlets (*The Female Advocate* and *The Female Preacher* by *Eugenia*) had been attributed to her, suggesting close textual associations, and therefore possible consultation between the authors. The poem is in the form of a dialogue between four characters: "Melissa" (who probably speaks as the persona of Chudleigh herself, as she was frequently referred to as "Marissa"); the uncouth and "irreverent" Sir John Brute (Chudleigh says: "Those expressions which I thought would be indecent in the Mouth of a Reverend Divine are spoken by Sir John Brute"); a Parson, and Sir William Loveall. In the poem Chudleigh/Melissa analyses the state of marriage and the female condition, her argument starting with the recognition that women "are generally less knowing and less Rational than the Men", but that "'tis oftener owing to the illness of our education than the weakness of our Capacities". This excerpt, which continues to the end of the poem, begins at its heart, when Melissa passionately asserts women's double-bind: as victims of male derision and as uneducated fools.

Lines 638–845
639. *Æsop's*: by tradition a slave in ancient Greece, 6th century B.C. and author of the *Fables*.
656. *Vines, nor Bays*: signs of achievement.

681. *Lucretia*: quintessentially virtuous wife of Tarquinius; her rape and ensuing suicide were the causes of the overthrow of the monarchy and establishment of the Roman Republic (see *The Resolution* line 225); *Porcia*: Portia, Roman woman of 1st century B.C., best known as the wife of Brutus, who after his death committed suicide herself.
682. *Cornelia*: remembered as the consummate virtuous Roman woman (ca.190–100 B.C.); devoted to her sons Tiberius and Gaius Gracchus.
683. *Zenobia*: a Syrian woman who lived in the 3rd century B.C. After her husband's death she became ruler of the Palmyrene empire and invaded Egypt; she became a prominent philosopher, socialite and Roman matron.
725. *Wool-sacks*: the wool-sack is the official seat of the Lord Chancellor in the House of Lords.
781. *Spaw*: spa.
783. *Æsculapius*: in Greek and Roman mythology, god of healing and medicine.
790. *Cring*: cringe.

Selected Bibliography

Collected Works
Margaret J.M. Ezell (ed.): *The Poems and Prose of Mary, Lady Chudleigh* (Oxford and New York: Oxford University Press, 1993).

Biographies
George Ballard, *Memoirs of Several Ladies of Great Britain who have been Celebrated for their Writings or Skill in the Learned Languages, Arts and Sciences* (1752), ed. Ruth Perry (Detroit: Wayne State University Press, 1985).

Anthologies
Robyn Bolam (ed.): *Eliza's Babes; Four Centuries of Women's Poetry in English, c. 1500–1900*—excerpt from *The Ladies Defence*, but inaccurate bibliographical reference to manuscripts by Chudleigh being held at the Huntingdon and Houghton Libraries (Tarset: Bloodaxe Books, 2005).

Criticism
Marilyn Williamson, *Raising Their Voices: British Women Writers, 1650–1750* (Detroit: Wayne State University Press, 1990).

Hilda Smith, *Reason's Disciples: Seventeenth-Century English Feminists* (Urbana, IL: University of Illinois Press, 1982).

Barbara Olive, *The Fabric of Restoration Puritanism: Mary Chudleigh's The Song of the Three Children Paraphras'd*, in Laura Lunger Knoppers, *Puritanism and its Discontents* (Newark, DE: University of Delaware Press, 2003).

www.ingramcontent.com/pod-product-compliance
Lightning Source LLC
Chambersburg PA
CBHW031150160426
43193CB00008B/316